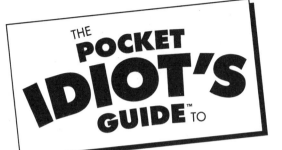

THE POCKET IDIOT'S GUIDE™ TO

the iPod

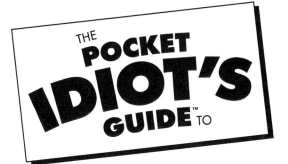

the iPod

by Damon Brown

ALPHA

A member of Penguin Group (USA) Inc.

ALPHA BOOKS

Published by the Penguin Group

Penguin Group (USA) Inc., 375 Hudson Street, New York, New York 10014, U.S.A.

Penguin Group (Canada), 10 Alcorn Avenue, Toronto, Ontario, Canada M4V 3B2 (a division of Pearson Penguin Canada Inc.)

Penguin Books Ltd, 80 Strand, London WC2R 0RL, England

Penguin Ireland, 25 St Stephen's Green, Dublin 2, Ireland (a division of Penguin Books Ltd)

Penguin Group (Australia), 250 Camberwell Road, Camberwell, Victoria 3124, Australia (a division of Pearson Australia Group Pty Ltd)

Penguin Books India Pvt Ltd, 11 Community Centre, Panchsheel Park, New Delhi—110 017, India

Penguin Group (NZ), cnr Airborne and Rosedale Roads, Albany, Auckland 1310, New Zealand (a division of Pearson New Zealand Ltd)

Penguin Books (South Africa) (Pty) Ltd, 24 Sturdee Avenue, Rosebank, Johannesburg 2196, South Africa

Penguin Books Ltd, Registered Offices: 80 Strand, London WC2R 0RL, England

Contents

Introduction

If you want to see the future of music, you just need to pay attention to the young kid bobbing his head on the train during the morning commute. Or watch the jogger running through the local park. Pay attention and you'll see them everywhere. Little white iPod headphones.

iPods are as ubiquitous in today's world as the 8-track, record player, and even the once-popular portable CD player were in the past. What makes them so cool? They are lightweight, can carry several thousand songs, and are cheap relative to their power. And you don't have to haul around your CDs anymore—your computer carries your whole CD collection, and the iPod becomes your portable listening station.

Even with all these benefits, the leap to using a digital music device can be intimidating. If you're nervous about purchasing an iPod or have one and can't make heads or tails of it, this book is for you.

In plain English, I show you …

- What iPods are out there.
- How to make your whole CD collection portable.
- Ways to download music straight to your iPod.
- Radio programming, photography, and other cool iPod uses.

And, most importantly, you'll be able to begin enjoying your iPod after reading a few quick pages. With this book by your side, there will be no reason for techies to have all the fun anymore.

About the Sidebars

You'll find four different sidebars throughout the book:

iTerms

These boxes define iPod-related terms that may be new to you.

Heads Up

These sidebars give you extra information to help you make the most of your iPod experience.

Crossed Wires

These boxes help you avoid technical problems you might run into.

Music to Your Ears

These sidebars contain fun facts about the iPod, music, or technology.

Acknowledgments

My thanks go first to the higher powers for giving me the gift of writing. Second, my mom, Bernadette Johnson, for inspiring me to be the best I can be. I also would like to thank my partner, Dr. Parul Jashbai Patel, for showing me her unconditional love, support, and respect.

All my mentors who taught me how to be a word warrior, particularly Jane Briggs Bunting, Stephen Garnett, Andrea King Collier, and, from back in the day, Mr. Crabb from Dwight Rich Middle and Ms. Farrell at Sexton High.

The agent who steered this book, Marilyn Allen (I loved working with you!), and prolific author Marcia Leyton Turner for helping make it happen. Also Michael Larsen, Manie Barron, and other people in the industry who have helped me along the way.

Also, thank you to the Alpha Books team behind this book, especially editors Renee Wilmeth, Mike Thomas, and Megan Douglass. And a special thanks to iPod aficionado Shana Naomi Krochmal for fact-checking.

To my family, from my dad, David Brown, to my Uncle George Johnson, for inspiring me to follow my own path. To little cousin A.J., my pride and joy: I hope to sneak a typewriter under your little baby hands. Also to A. Raymond Johnson, Deirdra Bishop, Kristie Keenon, Jeanette Hurt, Kurt Collins, and all my friends who have given their love and support to me and my writing. This is for you.

Finally, I'd like to thank my friends and mentors who have passed: Wilma Garcia, Dick Schwarzloze, and Shannon George. I feel your presence every day.

Trademarks

All terms mentioned in this book that are known to be or are suspected of being trademarks or service marks have been appropriately capitalized. Alpha Books and Penguin Group (USA) Inc. cannot attest to the accuracy of this information. Use of a term in this book should not be regarded as affecting the validity of any trademark or service mark.

Chapter 1

Different Personalities, Different iPods

In This Chapter

- The four kinds of iPods
- Which iPod should I get?
- Alarm clocks, text notes, and other goodies
- Song space for each model

If variety is the spice of life, then choosing your iPod is like eating a big pot of gumbo. This chapter goes over the four iPods and their endless features, from size and memory storage to play time and price. Armed with the details, you can choose the best one based on your money, space, and music collection—the Original iPod, iPod Mini/Nano, iPod Shuffle, or the Photo iPod.

First, an Overall Comparison

There are iPods for different lifestyles. Athletes may prefer the lightweight Shuffle, whereas music aficionados may like the large storage size offered by the iPod Photo. Here are the different models side by side.

iPod Models

	Original	Mini/Nano	Shuffle	Photo
List Price	$299	$199/$249	$99/$149	$349/$449
Weight	5.6 oz.	3.6 oz./1.5 oz.	.78 oz.	5.9/6.4 oz.
Memory	20 GB	4 or 6 GB/2 or 4 GB	512 MB/1 GB	30/60 GB
Songs	5,000	1,000 or 1,500/500 or 1,000	120/240	7,500/15,000
Battery	12 hours	18 hours/14 hours	12 hours	15 hours

Crossed Wires

Remember that you will be storing your main music library on your computer, so the iPod doesn't need to hold your whole collection. The iPod you purchase should be based on how much music you need to take with you on the road, not just on how much you have at home.

The Original

If you're not sure which iPod is best for you, the Original iPod is a good choice. It comes only in one music library size and only one color, white.

The Original iPod can carry up to 5,000 songs (20 GB of music library space). Five thousand songs might not sound like much, but that's equal to about 350 CDs. It enables you to take your music collection on the road with you wherever you go.

Unfortunately, it's not gonna fit in most pockets—that's what the Mini/Nano and the tiny Shuffle are best for. It's built like a solid pack of playing cards. You'll need to use the slide-on clip, included with the iPod, to attach it to your clothes.

It weighs in at around 6 ounces, so it's a noticeable weight if you want to jog with it on your clothes. Unless you don't mind carrying it in your hand, plan on buying an armband accessory to jog.

There are lots of music options on the Original iPod, though, making it much more attractive for control freaks than the Shuffle. Aside from random play, you can create your own *playlists* or organize your collection based on artist, album, song, genre, or composer.

iTerms

A **playlist** is kind of like a digital mix-tape, simply a list of your favorite songs fitting a particular theme. For instance, you might put all your favorite dance music into a playlist and call it Party Music 1.

The Original iPod is controlled by an Apple Touch Wheel, best described as a sensitive flat joystick. Pressing any primary direction will control the music; moving your thumb clockwise or counter-clockwise will adjust the volume or move you up and down the menus. There are no extra buttons.

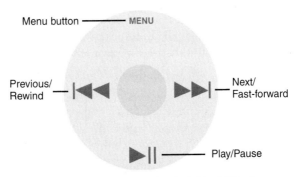

The iPod Photo and Mini also use the Apple Touch Wheel system.

The Original iPod can be used as a portable hard drive or backup for your computer files. For instance, if you've got a report you have to bring to your school or work computer, you can hook up your iPod on your home PC or Mac, save the document on the device, and retrieve it by hooking up the iPod to a computer again. It works similar to a flash drive, but is capable of transferring much bigger files.

Audiobooks, popular books read aloud by the authors or famous actors, are also playable on the Original iPod. You can buy them through the iTunes Music Store and other sites.

It also comes with a few pocket organizer programs. You can jot down grocery lists on text notes, check the calendar, or keep track of your contacts. An alarm clock and automatic shut-down timer are built in.

Heads Up

You can buy an accessory to store photos on your Original iPod, but it's easier to just get the iPod Photo in the first place if you think you'll be saving pictures.

The updated iPod Original released in summer 2005 has a nice color screen, but most models have a 2-inch black-and-white display. The Original iPod note programs aren't going to replace any pocket organizer you may have. However, even the black-and-white screens are crisp and detailed enough for all your music information, and it's still larger than the iPod Mini/Nano display (or the Shuffle, which simply doesn't have a screen). A backlight can be turned on and off.

The computer company HP also sells iPods. They are virtually the same, but the HP package only comes with iPod software for the PC. The traditional Apple package comes with both Mac and PC software. You can still buy the HP iPod if you're a Mac user, but you'll have to download the software from the Apple website. See Appendix C for more information.

The Mini

Despite the light weight, the iPod Mini/Nano has all the music options of the Original iPod. It supports all the music modes, such as random play, and also uses the Apple Touch Wheel controls.

Heads Up

iPods are white, but the Mini comes in four colors: blue, green, pink, and silver. The Nano comes in white and black.

Because of its slim figure, the Mini's screen is a bit smaller than the other iPods, 1.67 inches compared to 2 inches. Like the Original, the Minis released after summer 2005 have a color screen instead of a black-and-white. All models have a backlight function. The iPod Nano is a thinner iPod Mini introduced in summer 2005. It operates the same as the Mini.

The Shuffle

The iPod Shuffle is the simplest to use of all the models. You plug it into your computer, choose which songs you want on it, and hit the road.

Compared to other iPods, there isn't much control over your music experience while traveling. You can either play the songs in your Shuffle in order or play them randomly. That's pretty much it. There are neither homemade playlists nor any way to organize songs by category on the Shuffle.

However, you *can* tell the Shuffle what music to put on your iPod when you have it hooked up to your computer. For instance, if you're in a jazzy mood, you can ask the Shuffle to fill your iPod only with music from the Jazz genre. Or you can tell it to transfer music randomly from your favorite playlists.

It doesn't have an Apple Touch Wheel. Instead, the Shuffle uses a tiny controller to adjust volume and stop and start songs.

There really isn't any memory space to use the Shuffle as temporary storage of your computer files except for, say, a Microsoft Word document or two. On the positive side, no connection cord is required to transfer files—just plug it directly into your computer. There is no screen display, so you have to guess what you're listening to. There are no menus, nor any pocket organizer programs such as Calendar or Alarm Clock/Sleep.

The Photo

The iPod Photo has the standard music options and Apple Touch Wheel controls, but has more space and battery life than most other models. The cheaper iPod Photo, which is 30 GB, has 50 percent more space than Original iPod. The more expensive 60 GB iPod Photo has three times the Original's memory— meaning you can carry about three times the music.

The extra space really comes in handy when you start downloading photos to your iPod Photo. You can take any pictures on your computer, transfer them to your iPod, and use the device as a picture viewer on the road.

Heads Up

The iPod Photo is compatible with every major digital photo format: JPEG, BMP, GIF, TIFF, PSD, and PNG. You shouldn't have a problem viewing any of your digital pictures.

You can also do a slideshow by buying the AV cable and hooking up your iPod Photo to a TV or projector, making this iPod perfect for impromptu family reunions.

Photos look good on the iPod Photo's 2-inch color screen, as does the smoother, sleeker menu font. The only model with the color display, the iPod Photo is well suited to do pocket organizer functions such as Calendar, Text Notes, and Contacts. Even the little mini-games such as Solitare look better in color. Unlike the black-and-white iPods, it doesn't need a backlight.

The Least You Need to Know

- iPods can hold up to 15,000 songs.
- The average battery power is 15 hours.
- Most iPods just have a touchpad—no buttons.
- Unlike other models, the Shuffle has no screen.
- iPod prices range from $99 to $449.

iTunes

In This Chapter

- Finding and playing music
- Creating your own playlists
- Burning mix CDs
- Playing the radio

iTunes—the software program used with all iPods—is the virtual jukebox that will play all your music. Everything you want to do with your iPod can be done through this handy interface. iTunes also enables you to stream radio stations through an Internet connection, making the program as sophisticated as the CD player you've got on the shelf.

Playing Your Music

The upper-left corner of iTunes is similar to your traditional CD player. The large forward arrow plays your current selection. When the music plays, the arrow turns into a double bar, and you can use it to pause the music. The double arrows forward skip to the next selection. The double arrows going back restart the track or, with a double-click, go to the previous selection. The long bar below the icons controls the volume. Drag the circle along the line to adjust the sound.

Heads Up

Apple regularly updates the iPod software, including iTunes, and will inform you when a new version is available online. Follow the instructions to download the update onto your computer.

Volume and   Music   Search   Browse
play options   info   bar   icon

Album art

The iTunes interface.

Heads Up

You can also double-click a song to play it. You can still use the play icons to control the music.

The face panel next to the play icons gives you information about the song currently playing. The very top cycles between showing the song title, album, and artist. Below the song info, iTunes lists the song time—you can shuffle between listing remaining time, elapsed time, and total time by clicking the information. The long bar below the time shows visually how much play time remains. Like the volume controls, you can slide the diamond along the line to move to different parts of the song. The little triangle to the left of the song information switches your face plate between song info and a cool visual equalizer.

Icons

Along the bottom of your iTunes interface is a group of colorful icons. From creating playlists to random music selection, these are quick ways to tailor your music experience.

iTunes Icons

Type	What It Does
Plus/Wheel Symbol	Creates a playlist
Two Arrows Twisting	Switches random play on and off
Two Arrows Circling	Repeats songlist, repeat song, no repeat
Downward Arrow	Shows or hides album art
Box with Arrows	Shows video full screen (if applicable)
iPod	Modifies iPod settings (when plugged in)
Three Bars	Opens music equalizer window
Star	Turns on music visual display
Eject	Ejects CD

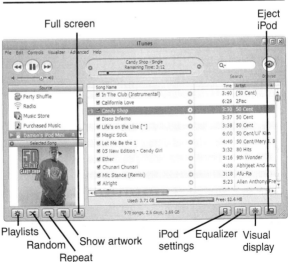

iTunes has several icons for quick navigation.

Song Information

Select a particular song and, moving right from the left-hand song title, you'll see all the pertinent song information.

iTunes Song Information

Information Column	What It Means
Song Name	Title
Time	Total song length
Artist	Performer
Album	CD title
Genre	Music format
My Rating	Your song rating (if any)
Play Count	How many times the song has played
Last Played	Date and time of the last play

For more detailed song information, use the Get Info option. Go over the song title and right-click (on the PC) or hold the mouse button (on the Mac). Select the Get Info option. Alternatively, you can click the File menu at the very top and select Get Info.

Along with the basic information, Get Info shows the actual song location in your computer directory, composer data, and other information. You can also increase or decrease the volume of that particular song if the CD burned was too loud or soft, or trim the beginning or ending of the song.

Party Shuffle

The Party Shuffle enables you to play a random list of songs from your library or from specific playlists. Party Shuffle sets iTunes to replay so that you never have to restart the music.

Start by clicking the Party Shuffle icon in the left column. A list of songs will display. At the bottom of the list of songs are different criteria you can use to modify your list. Pulling down the Source menu enables you to make a random list from songs other than your library. For instance, if you've made a playlist with all your favorite slow jazz songs called Slow Jazz 1, you can scroll down the Source menu and tell iTunes to play random songs from that list.

Adjust the Display options to show the most recently played songs and the upcoming songs. A box below the Source list can be checked that will make iTunes play your higher-rated songs more often.

Rating Your Music

iTunes lets you rate each song within your library. Songs are rated on a scale between one and five stars. There are no default ratings for your songs.

To rate a particular song, follow these steps:

1. Find the song in your library.
2. Move your cursor along the song information row until you reach the My Rating column (between Genre and Play Count).
3. Click the My Rating column.

4. You will see five dots. Move your cursor over the dot that corresponds to the rating you want to give.

5. Click the mouse button when you get your desired rating.

Heads Up _____

You can also rate your songs directly on your iPod Original, Mini/Nano, or Photo. Check out Chapter 5 for more information.

Finding Music

There are three ways to find music in your iTunes library:

- Music Search
- Browsing
- Manually

Music Search

The Search bar is located in the upper-right area of your iTunes. Type in certain words, and iTunes will list the songs that fit that criteria. For instance, if you only want Billy Joel songs, click the Search bar, type in "Billy Joel," and all Billy Joel-related songs display. Press the small X on the right of the Search bar to end the search.

The Search bar looks for words through all the song information, meaning that it would not only list songs where Billy Joel was artist, but also any songs that list him as composer, writer, or in any other capacity. It also means that if some random group has a song title that contains "Billy Joel," it pops up on the list, too. For more control, click the magnifying glass symbol and specify whether you want to use the criteria to search for artists, albums, composers, songs, or all variables. Any more detail requires using the Browse function.

Browsing

The Browse icon is the eye symbol in the upper-right corner. Click Browse, and iTunes opens up a new panel underneath the song information. Here, all your music is organized by Genre, Artist, and Album. Scroll down the various lists and click specific criteria to find what you want. For instance, if you're in the mood for Alternative music, go to Genre and click Alternative. iTunes will list all the music labeled as Alternative. Then you can scroll down the other columns to find a specific artist or album within the Alternative genre. Clicking the All item at the top of each lists removes the selected criteria and expands your search. You can click the Browse eye again to close the Browsing function.

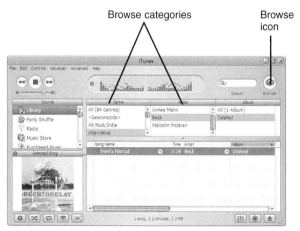

Browse categories

Browse icon

Using iTunes Browse function.

Manually

iTunes lists all your music by Song Name, Time, Artist, and Album. The default is to list your library alphabetically by title, but you can click the column labels to organize your music by a particular criterion. Then you can scroll up or down and find the songs you want. Clicking an already highlighted column label puts the music in reverse order—Z–A in the Song Name, Artist, or Album column, from longest to shortest in the Time column.

Heads Up _____

iTunes organizes artists by first name, last name—not by last name, first name.

Creating Playlists

With playlists you can group your favorite songs under one heading. For instance, a playlist you name Exercise Mix 1 may have all your favorite jogging songs.

Basic Playlist

Go under File, and click New Playlist. A new playlist called Untitled Playlist will display in the left column, below Library, Party Shuffle, and other iTunes items. You can now type in a name for your playlist. Don't worry—if you decide to change the playlist title later, you can double-click the name and change it another time.

Playlists allow you to make your own music mix.

Now click the Library (or another playlist, if that's where you plan on getting the music from) and find the first song you want to add to your new playlist. Put your cursor over the song, hold down the mouse button, and manually drag the song to where your new playlist is listed in the left column. Then just repeat the process until your playlist is complete. Remember that you're not dealing with CDs or another limited medium, so your playlist can be as long as you like.

Heads Up

Your playlist song order isn't set in stone. Just pick a song you want to move, drag it up or down your list of playlist songs, and drop it where you like.

Smart Playlist

Creating basic playlists manually can be a lot of work. Luckily, Apple included smart playlists that essentially do the work for you.

Go under File, and click New Smart Playlist. An info box will appear. Here you can tell iTunes what criteria you want it to use to create your new playlist. The criterion is based on item, relationship, and description. For instance, you can do Artist (item) Contains (relationship) "Billy Joel" (description). The smart playlist will then create a playlist featuring all songs listing Billy Joel as the artist. Unlike the Search function, the smart playlist won't include songs where Billy Joel was listed as composer or any other position other than artist.

Alternatively, if you want everything but songs that feature Billy Joel, you can do Artist (item) Does Not Contain (relationship) "Billy Joel" (description). This will make a playlist with all the songs not featuring Billy Joel.

To get more specific, you may add more playlist descriptions by clicking the Plus button to the right of the initial criterion. For instance, if you want a playlist of all your Billy Joel songs, but don't want to include his duet with Ray Charles, your first request would read Artist (item) Contains (relationship) "Billy Joel" (description) and your second request would read Artist (item) Does Not Contain (relationship) "Ray Charles" (description). With multiple requests, you can tell iTunes to add songs that match All or Any of the criteria, an option that can be selected in the small column at the top of the smart playlist box.

Like the basic playlist, your smart playlist can be as long as you like. However, you can't control the order of the songs listed in it—only the criteria of the songs chosen. For variety, you can toggle the highlighted Time, Album, or another column to organize songs by time, chronological order, and so forth.

Item box
Relationship box
Description box
Add or delete criteria

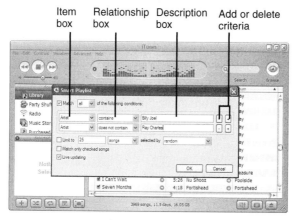

Smart playlists create mixes for you.

Burning CDs

You can share your playlists with others by burning
a CD. Highlight your playlist and the Browse icon
in the upper-right corner turns into a Burn Disc
icon. Put a blank CD into your computer, click
Burn Disc, and iTunes will make a copy of your
playlist on CD.

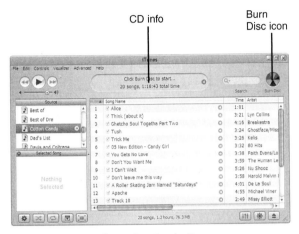

You can burn CDs of your favorite playlists.

Burning Tips

CD-R or CD-RW CDs work best, and packs with multiple CDs are available at most technology stores and even some drugstores. The average CD holds 78 minutes of music. If you have more than that in your playlist, you will have to create a shorter list or divide it among multiple discs (iTunes will alert you if this is required). The total playlist time is shown at the bottom of iTunes when the playlist is highlighted.

Crossed Wires _____

Be sure to make a backup copy of your music! Read Chapter 9 to learn how.

Getting Album Art

Unfortunately, although iTunes can automatically detect most artist and song information, it does not download the album cover art for you, unless you purchase the songs through the iTunes store. You have to get it yourself. When you get the album art, it will appear in the lower-left corner whenever you select a song from the CD.

To get album art, follow these steps:

1. Get on the Internet.
2. Use a search engine such as Yahoo! or Google and type in the album name.
3. Find a website with the album art.
4. Right-click the picture on PC, or hold the mouse button on Mac, and choose Save Picture As.
5. Save the picture on your computer, in the same area as your music files if possible.
6. Open iTunes and downsize the iTunes window so it only takes up part of the screen.
7. Find the album art on your computer.
8. Click and drag the album art into the lower-left corner where it says Drag Album Artwork Here.

Heads Up

iTunes automatically gives you album art when you purchase a single or album from the Apple Music Store.

Radio

The radio function hooks you into online music stations around the world. Imagine your car radio picking up frequencies from Japan, Brazil, and the UK.

To use the iTunes radio function, you must first make sure your computer is connected to the Internet. Then click the Radio icon in the left column, right under Party Shuffle. A list of available genres will appear, such as Blues, Classical, and Hard Rock.

Clicking a particular genre unfolds the list of radio stations available. Each station lists its program title, sound quality, and program description. Double-click the title or highlight the program and press the Play icon to start the music. They usually take a second or two to start up because the music must be downloaded from the Internet. When it begins, the current song information is listed in the face panel along with the radio station's web address. The radio programs are not stored on your hard drive.

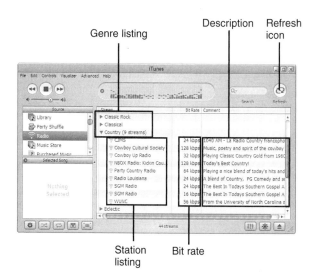

The iTunes Radio picks up stations from around the globe.

Crossed Wires

Programs sometimes are temporarily offline, so move on to another program if the music hasn't started within a minute.

Click the Refresh icon, located in the upper-right corner where the Browse icon used to be, regularly to see whether any new stations have become available since you started your iTunes session.

The Least You Need to Know

- iTunes music controls are similar to a CD player.
- Press the column heads to organize songs by that topic.
- Playlists are homemade mixes you create.
- Burn your playlists through iTunes.

From CD to iPod

In This Chapter

- Get your music on your computer
- Transfer your CD collection to your iPod
- Organize your digital music collection
- Access all the music currently on your computer

The iPod enables you to take your music on the go, perhaps even your whole CD collection. This chapter shows you the easiest way to transfer your music stash to your iPod.

Transferring Your Music

Transferring your favorite music from CD to iPod can be done in minutes. Here's how.

Move CD Music to iTunes

First, make sure your computer is connected to the Internet—this allows iTunes to automatically list the track information for nearly any CD you put in. This way, you won't have to type out the song information.

Put the CD in your computer drive and, after a moment, iTunes will look up the track information for you. The CD with the full track listing will appear in iTunes. In the upper-right corner, the Import icon replaces the Browse icon. Click the Import icon to copy your whole CD into iTunes. If you only want to copy a specific song, click that song title and then click Import.

Transfer your CDs to iTunes by clicking the Import button.

The computer will then transfer your CD to iTunes. It can take several minutes depending on your computer CD drive and computer speed—the face panel shows the amount of time left, and a bell rings to let you know it's done. Now the music is part of your iTunes library.

Heads Up

If you can't get online when you are copying a CD, wait until you get online, highlight the track names you need, go to the Advanced heading at the top of the iTunes interface, and then Get CD Track Names.

If you decide against keeping the music, find the song, click the title, and press Delete on the keyboard. Doing so completely removes the song from your computer.

Heads Up

If you don't have the time or energy, you can use a digital transfer company such as Get Digital (www.getdigitalinc.com). You mail them your CDs and they convert them into iPod files for you.

Move iTunes Music to iPod

Connect your iPod to your computer. You do so via a USB or FireWire cord or, with the Shuffle, by directly connecting the unit to your computer port. An iPod icon will show up right below purchased music. If it is your first time using it, Apple asks you to register the device.

If any songs are on your iPod, a list of them will now appear in iTunes. At the bottom, you'll find information on the remaining space available on your iPod, as well as the number of songs and hours (or days!) of music available.

Transferring music to your iPod is the same process as creating your playlist. Go to Library and find music you want to add to your iPod. Click the song title, drag the music into the left column over your iPod symbol, and release to add it to your iPod collection.

You can also automatically update your iPod with all your music files or only with music not already on it. To do this, modify your iPod Preferences, under the Edit menu. Read more about this in Chapter 9.

iPod
icon

Drag your favorite songs onto your iPod through iTunes.

Heads Up

Want to add a whole playlist? Just highlight the playlist name on the left side and click and drag it onto your iPod.

Delete music by clicking your iPod symbol on the left side, finding the song you want to remove, and pressing the Delete button on the keyboard. Doing so only removes the song from your iPod, not your computer.

If You Already Have Music on Your Computer

When you run iTunes for the first time, your computer will ask you if you'd like it to find previous music folders on your computer. Say "Yes," and it will automatically add your current music.

If for some reason you say "No," you can always manually transfer it later. First, open the iTunes program and move it so that it is available on one section of your computer screen. Next, find the area on your computer where your music files are stored—you can search for "mp3" or "wav" if you're having trouble locating them. Then you can highlight the music you want to transfer and click and drag the files into the iTunes program. iTunes takes a second or two to read each music file before adding it to your library.

> **Crossed Wires** _____
>
> Don't delete the original music file after adding it to iTunes! It still needs the file to play the song.

Organize Your Music Collection

Here are some tips to keep your music collection in order:

- Always add your CD music through iTunes, not through other computer programs. This allows for cleaner organization because all your music will be saved in the same area on your computer.

- Delete your music through iTunes, not directly from your hard drive. If not done through the music program, iTunes will still list the now-unplayable track, and you have to delete it in iTunes anyway.

- Find track names through iTunes. Typing them in yourself is an error-prone practice, not to mention a tiring one. But if you're importing a mix made by a friend, you may have to do it the long way.

The Least You Need to Know

- iTunes will automatically download song info of CDs you put in.
- Independent companies will transfer your CD collection to iTunes for you.
- Drag and drop music over your iPod icon to transfer it.
- iTunes will find your previously stored music.

Chapter 4

The Apple Music Store

In This Chapter

- Downloading music on your computer
- Finding music online
- Limitations of music use
- How to download audiobooks

iTunes enables you to buy music in digital form, ready to go onto your iPod, through the Apple Music Store. This chapter shows you how to download music from the store, what you need to know about digital music, and the limitations of digital music use.

Downloading from the Internet (*Legally*)

In 2003, Apple started the Apple Music Store, the first successful paid online music service. Within 16 days, there were more than 2 million song purchases, one at a time, for a dollar a pop.

The best part about the Apple Music Store is that you can buy a whole album (usually for $9.99) or just one song of an album ($.99). It eliminates the need to buy an entire CD just because you like one or two particular songs.

Getting Music

To use the Apple Music Store, you need iTunes, an e-mail address, an active credit card, and an Internet connection.

Heads Up

Apple also sells Apple Music Store gift certificates worth up to $200.

Setting Up Your Store Account

Click the Music Store icon in the left column. iTunes will ask you whether you want to set up an account. You then provide iTunes with an e-mail address, password, and credit card of your choice. These preliminaries lead you to the Apple Music Store front page.

Finding What You Want

The Apple Music Store front page updates regularly with new releases, top song download listings, and exclusive iTunes-only tracks (songs not available on CD). Clicking any of the song titles brings you to the music download screen. The front page also features audiobooks, music videos, and other multimedia for download.

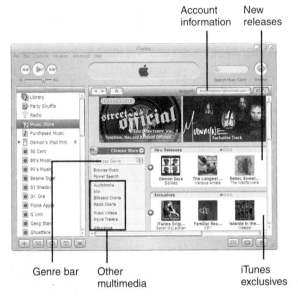

The Apple Music Store front page shows the hottest music available for download.

You can list songs by genre by clicking the Choose Genre button. It's located on the upper-left side of the front page.

You can also search the music store using the Search bar in the upper-right corner to type in your favorite artist or song. Searches list the top albums, songs, and artists related to your criterion at the top, and list every related song on the bottom half of the iTunes screen. Each song lists its title, playing time, artist, album, relevance, and song price. Double-clicking a song or highlighting it and pressing the Play icon gives you a 30-second snippet.

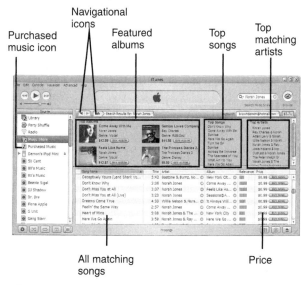

Navigational icons

Purchased music icon

Featured albums

Top songs

Top matching artists

All matching songs

Price

Songs can be found in several different ways at the Apple Music Store.

Use the back arrow in the upper-left corner of the Apple Music Store to go to the previous query and the nearby Home symbol to go back to the front page. The other side of the screen shows the current account, e-mail and, if it is a gift certificate, the money remaining in the account.

Clicking Buy Song or Buy Album will download the item into your iTunes library. The cost will be subtracted from your account.

Heads Up _____

All your tunes from the Apple Music Store are listed under the Purchased Music icon.

Limits of Use

To thwart piracy, songs purchased through the Apple Music Store can be played on a maximum of five different computers. When you give one of your downloaded songs to a buddy, iTunes asks you whether you want to allow his or her computer to be one of the authorized computers.

However, if you just want to *play* a song on your friend's computer, hook up your iPod to his or her computer, find your song in the computer's iTunes, and play it. The song is automatically removed after you disconnect your iPod.

Gifts and Allowances

The Apple Music Store also lets you use prepaid cards and to send gift certificates and allowances through iTunes.

Redeeming Prepaid Cards

Mostly a promotional tool, prepaid cards can be found in products from Pepsi, 7-Eleven, and other vendors. You can redeem them through iTunes.

To redeem a prepaid card, follow these steps:

1. Click the Music Store icon in the left column.
2. Click Prepaid Cards, located in the left column of the Apple Music Store by Gift Certificates and Allowances.
3. Type in the 16-digit code on the back of your prepaid card.

Buying and Redeeming Gift Certificates

Gift certificates are the same as prepaid cards, but they don't have to be physical. You can choose to have a certificate sent to the gift recipient, but you can also e-mail it to them.

To send a gift certificate, follow these steps:

1. Click the Music Store icon in the left column.
2. Click Gift Certificates, located in the left column of the Apple Music Store by Allowances and Prepaid Cards.
3. Click Buy Now.
4. Choose between Emailing, Printing, or Mailing the gift certificate.

If you choose to e-mail, Apple will ask for your name, the recipient's name, and the recipient's e-mail. You can give an amount between $10 and $200 and include a personal message. It will send the gift certificate right away.

Crossed Wires

Apple sends the gift certificate as soon as you purchase it, so be sure to wait to purchase until the day you want the person to receive the gift.

If you decide to print the gift certificate, Apple will ask for your name, the recipient's name, and the gift certificate amount, from $10 to $200. You can also write a two-line personal message. Apple provides a document you can print yourself.

If you decide to mail it using the United States Postal Service, Apple will connect you to a special page. From there you provide your name and the recipient's name, the gift certificate amount, from $10 to $200, and a personal message. Then you give the recipient's full address for mailing.

To redeem a gift certificate, follow these steps:

1. Click the Music Store icon in the left column.
2. Click Gift Certificates, located in the left column of the Apple Music Store by Allowances and Prepaid Cards.
3. Click Redeem.
4. Enter the code listed on your gift certificate.

You can then use your gift certificate just like a credit card. Apple deducts from the gift certificate as you make music purchases. If you try to make a purchase totaling more than what remains on the gift certificate, Apple deducts the remaining balance from your listed credit card.

Creating an Allowance

The Apple Music Store also lets you create an allowance so that others can purchase iTunes music without having to have your credit card information at hand.

To set up an allowance, follow these steps:

1. Click the Music Store icon in the left column.

2. Click Allowance, located in the left column of the Apple Music Store by Gift Certificates and Prepaid Cards.

3. Type in your name and the recipient's name.

4. Choose a monthly allowance between $10 and $200.

5. Decide whether they should receive the first installment now or on the first of the next month.

6. Type in the recipient's Apple/iTunes ID or, if they don't have one, create a new one for them.

7. Type in a message for them if you like.

Apple then deducts your credit card when a new allowance is given at the first of every following month. You can give the allowance to the person right away if you wish. But if you're making arrangements after the twentieth of the month, Apple automatically waits until the first of the next month.

The Least You Need to Know

- You need iTunes, e-mail, Internet, and a credit card to use the Apple Music Store.
- Singles are $.99, albums usually $9.99.
- Audiobooks, music videos, and other multimedia are available.
- You can play purchased music only on five different computers.
- Apple Music Store offers prepaid cards, gift certificates, and monthly allowances.

iPod Original and Mini/Nano

In This Chapter

- Using your iPod Original or Mini/Nano
- Organizing your iPod music
- Cool extra functions
- Differences between the two models

The iPod Original and Mini/Nano are identical in controls and functions. This chapter will have you creating playlists, organizing music, and playing fun, included games in no time.

Your iPod Controls

Unlike bulky tape and CD players, you only need a thumb to control the iPod. It is made for one-hand use.

Apple Touch Wheel

Your iPod uses the Apple Touch Wheel. Older iPod Original models have four buttons between the wheel and screen: Previous/Rewind, Menu, Next/ Fast-Forward, and Play/Pause. All other Original models and iPod Mini/Nanos have these four buttons in the cardinal positions of the touch wheel. In the center is the Select button. You only need a thumb to control the iPod.

> ### Music to Your Ears
>
> The first iPods combined Apple Touch Wheel with buttons, but Apple removed all the extra buttons to save space when it made the iPod Mini. Because it became so popular, Apple eliminated the buttons on the Original iPods, too.

Press the Select button to "awaken" your iPod. A brief Apple logo will appear or, if you had a recent session, your last menu option will pop up. The top of the screen shows the time and a battery indicating the energy your iPod currently has.

Put your thumb lightly at the top of the touch wheel, where it says Menu in the later models. Now gently move your thumb around the wheel clockwise. Doing so moves the selected menu option down. Rotating your thumb around the wheel counterclockwise moves the current menu option up. When controlling any of the meters— say, for volume—clockwise means increase, counterclockwise means decrease.

Heads Up

The lighter you touch the Apple Touch
Wheel, the more responsive and accurate
it is.

The Buttons

Rotating your thumb lightly over the wheel adjusts
the menu or meter settings, but tapping the marked
area over a particular button activates it.

Tapping the Menu button returns you to the higher
set of menu options, and is similar to a "back" button
in an Internet browser. For instance, the Playlist
option is one of the menu features under Music.
Pressing the Menu button while highlighting Playlist
takes you to the Music option. Holding down the
Menu button turns your backlight on or off.

The Previous/Rewind, Next/Fast-Forward, and
Play/Pause buttons operate just like a CD player.
Tapping the Previous/Rewind button restarts the
current track, tapping it twice skips you to the previous song (if any), and holding it down rewinds
you quickly through the current song. Tapping the
Next/Fast-Forward button skips to the next track,
while holding it down fast-forwards you through
the current song.

The Select button confirms the current menu option.
And you hold down the Play/Pause button for a
few seconds to turn your iPod off. It will turn off
automatically after a short period of time.

On Your iPod

Like other Apple products, the iPod is a compact, deceptively simple device that is more versatile than it seems. Here is a tour of the different slots and switches.

Hold Switch

Located at the top of your iPod, the Hold switch prevents you from accidentally pressing a button while you're listening to music. Slide the switch to activate it. When the switch is set to hold, you will see an orange line, and the click wheel and select button will be deactivated.

Remote Port

Next to the Hold switch is the Remote port. Plug the optional remote headphones in here. The remote headphones are just like the regular iPod headphones, except they come with a small switch that has all the Apple Touch Wheel buttons on it. The remote headphones are sold separately.

Headphones Port

Plug your headphones into the Headphones port, located right next to the Remote port. The iPod accepts all $\frac{1}{8}$ headphones, so any earphones you've used for portable tape or CD players will work fine.

Heads Up _____

Speakers specially made for portable music systems also plug into the Headphones port.

Music on Your iPod

With the iPod you can find music using different categories and pull playlists created on your iTunes. You can also make your own playlists on the fly.

Heads Up _____

Later-generation Original iPods have an additional "Shuffle Songs" option that will mix up your tunes for you. This is available on the top menu.

Finding Your Music

On the top menu, you'll find listed Music, Extras, Settings, and Backlight—if you are in one of the submenus, tap the Menu button until you reach the described area. Scroll to Music and press the Select button.

You now can list your iPod catalog in alphabetic order based on the following:

- Playlists
- Artists

- Albums
- Songs
- Genre
- Composers
- Audiobooks

Press the Select option once to choose a method of order, and you will see the respective list. Then scroll up and down to find a deeper detail. For instance, clicking Artists, then Norah Jones may pull up two of her albums, requiring you to choose which album to play. With the exception of playlists and audiobooks, catalogs have an All option that enables you to play all the music performed under that particular artist, album, genre, composer, or list of songs.

Playlists

Playlists created in iTunes can be played on your iPod. If you have your iPod set to automatic update (selected by going to the Edit menu, then Preferences, and clicking on the iPod tab), you don't have to do anything to transfer it to your iPod—the computer will automatically add it. To manually add a new playlist to your iPod, just highlight the playlist name on the left side, and click and drag it onto your iPod symbol. Your iPod transfers all the music within the playlist, and the playlist name will now appear under the Playlist menu the next time you use your iPod.

Your iPod icon   Playlist name

Drag your favorite playlists to the iPod icon.

Crossed Wires

The iPod creates only a partial playlist if you don't have the room to transfer all the songs on your list.

You can also create temporary On-The-Go playlists right on your iPod. Find a song you like, highlight the title, and hold down the Select button. The song title will flash briefly, showing that it is now added to your On-The-Go playlist. Keep adding songs until you're done. Then go back to the Playlist menu (under Music) and select On-The-Go to listen to your playlist.

The iPod keeps your On-The-Go playlist even when the power is off. However, continuing the On-The-Go playlist process after restarting your iPod will start a new On-The-Go playlist—called, for instance, On-The-Go 2.

To delete your playlists, go to On-The-Go (under Playlist), and then click Clear Playlist. If you want to save the playlist, the next time you sync your iPod it will be copied to your iTunes program. Rename the playlist (Jogging replaces On-The-Go 1).

Rate Your Music

You can rate your music on your iPod, not only in the iTunes program. Songs are rated on a scale between one and five stars. There are no default ratings for your songs.

To rate a particular song, follow these steps:

1. Find the song.
2. Play the song.
3. Press the Menu button until you reach the top menu. (Music will be the top option.)
4. Highlight the Now Playing option and press Select.
5. Click the Select button two more times.
6. Move your Apple Touch Wheel left and right to highlight fewer or more stars.
7. Click the Select button when you get your desired ratings.

Crossed Wires

iTunes treats ratings done on the computer and done on the iPod separately! To get consistent ratings, either transfer your iPod rated song back to your song library or move your iTunes-rated song onto the iPod to replace the previous.

Recharging Your iPod

There are two ways to recharge your iPod: through the computer and directly through a wall outlet.

Through the Computer

To recharge through the computer, use the included USB cable or, if you have only space for a FireWire connection, purchase the optional FireWire cable. The wide end connects to the iPod. Press the small, oblong indentations in on the wire plug— you will see the tiny metal hooks near the end of the wire disappear. Now, while still pressing the indentations in, slide the wire into your Dock Connector port, located at the very bottom of your iPod. Make sure the top of the wire plug is facing the front of the iPod—the wire plug top has a small icon, a box with a line inside of it. When it is fully inside, let go of the indentations and make sure the plug is snug.

If your computer is on, it should acknowledge the connection and load your iTunes program if it hasn't already been started. Your iPod screen will then say "Do not disconnect," and the small battery icon will begin a filling animation. The animation stops when your iPod is fully recharged.

> **Crossed Wires** _____
>
> Most computers can only recharge the iPod when the computer is actually on.

Using the Wall Plug

Alternatively, you can use the included battery plug to connect your iPod to a wall outlet. Use the same wire plug method to connect it to the battery plug.

> **Heads Up** _____
>
> If time's short, you can always do a partial charge. A couple hours will give you 80 percent power; 3 to 5 hours will give you 100 percent power.

Settings

The settings are vast, but the iPod remembers your preferences, so you won't need to reset them every time you start a new music session.

The Settings menu is the on the top menu, available when you first power up your iPod.

iPod Settings

About	iPod info such as songs and remaining space
Main Menu	Allows you to modify what is listed on the menu
Shuffle	Select between song, album, or no shuffling
Repeat	Select between one, all songs, or no repeating
Backlight Timer	Have backlight shut off after a certain time
Audiobooks	Control talking speed of audiobooks
EQ	Choose between two dozen equalizer settings
Sound Check	Maintain equal volume among all songs played back, regardless of their recorded volume
Contrast	Lighten or darken your screen display
Clicker	Have iPod make a noise when you move the menu bar
Date & Time	Set time zone, date, time, and 12- or 24-hour clock
Contacts	Choose sorting method of contacts
Language	Select your iPod display language
Legal	Apple copyright information
Reset All Settings	Go to default factory settings

The Least You Need to Know

- The Original and Mini/Nano are identical except for size and capacity.
- The Hold Switch prevents accidental button presses.
- You can find your music seven different ways.
- Drag and drop playlists on iPod icon to add.
- On-The-Go lists are playlists you make directly on your iPod.

Chapter 6

The iPod Shuffle

In This Chapter

- Using your Shuffle
- Selecting Shuffle music
- Transferring music to the Shuffle

The iPod Shuffle is the most straightforward of the iPods—you just plug it into your computer, let it download your songs, and hit the road. This chapter shows you how to make the most of this 1-ounce device.

Your iPod Shuffle Controls

Unlike the other iPods, the Shuffle has no display screen and does not use the Apple Touch Wheel; instead, you use a simple set of controls on the front and back of the device.

> ♫ **Music to Your Ears** _____
>
> The Shuffle's dimensions are about 3 inches by 1 inch, smaller than 5 sticks of gum.

Using the Front Controller

The front of your iPod Shuffle has four buttons surrounding a small circular pad. Going clockwise, they are Volume up, Next track, Volume down, and Previous track. In the center is Play/Pause.

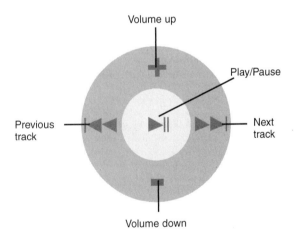

The Shuffle controller differs from the other iPods.

Press the Play/Pause button for three seconds to hold; doing so prevents any random button presses from affecting the player, just like the Hold switch on the other iPods. A small light indicator above the controller will change from green to orange.

Press the Play/Pause button for three seconds again to unhold. The light will change back to green.

Using the Back Controller

On the back you'll find the Play Order switch and the Battery Status button/light.

The Play Order switch has three positions: Off, Repeat, and Shuffle. Repeat plays the current list of songs, in order, and continuously repeats the list until you turn off the player. Shuffle mixes up the current list, randomizing your songs. Slide the switch up and down to change the mode. And remember, no matter which mode you're in, you can always skip a song by pressing the Next button.

Crossed Wires

Unlike the other iPods, remember to turn the switch to Off when the Shuffle isn't in use.

Just below the switch is the Battery Status button/light. Pressing the button shows you the battery status.

iPod Shuffle Battery Indicator

Light Color	Means
Green	Plenty of power left
Amber	Low on power
Red	Needs to be recharged ASAP
No light	Out of power

Nothing happens to your music if the Shuffle runs out of battery power. It just shuts down.

Music on Your iPod

The Shuffle transfers music a little bit differently than the other iPods. There are no playlists on your Shuffle, nor any way to select specific songs on-the-fly. You decide which music you want on the Shuffle on your computer, not on the iPod itself. Here's how.

Finding Your Music

At the bottom of your iPod Shuffle is a detachable end with a USB plug underneath. Remove the end and put the USB plug directly into your computer's USB port. The computer makes a ding noise to indicate that the iPod is connected.

The Shuffle begins automatically downloading random songs from your Library—approximately 240 with the 1 GB model and 120 with the smaller, 512 MB model. A yellow light at the far end of the

Shuffle front begins blinking, a sign that the iPod is being loaded with songs. It stops blinking when the loading is done.

Crossed Wires

Don't just take the Shuffle out after it starts blinking! You still need to press the iTunes Eject button to remove it the proper way.

Choosing Your Songs

If you don't like the selection of songs, press the Autofill button in the bottom menu to have it pick another batch of random songs. Next to the Autofill button, where it says Autofill from:, you can choose a specific playlist from which you want it to make a random selection. For instance, if you have a 300-song playlist called Jogging Tunes, you can plug your Shuffle in every morning, specify that it autofill from Jogging Tunes, and it will pick 120 or 240 random songs for your daily jog.

Three other options, Choose songs randomly, Choose higher rated songs more often, and Replace all songs when autofilling, may be checked on or off.

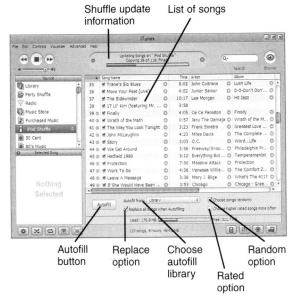

Shuffle update information   List of songs

Autofill button   Replace option   Choose autofill library   Rated option   Random option

By default, iTunes automatically loads up your Shuffle with random songs.

Shuffle Equipment

With no Apple Touch Wheel or screen, the Shuffle has a basic design compared to the other, more sophisticated iPods. There is only one port and one included extra.

Headphones Port

You'll find the Headphones port at the very top of the device. Remote headphones aren't compatible with the Shuffle, but any other basic headphones are.

Lanyard

You can use the lanyard to hang the Shuffle around your neck. Connect it by removing the Shuffle's end, as you would when connecting it to the computer, and snapping it into the lanyard holder.

Crossed Wires

Make sure you hear the lanyard make a proper "snap" before you start running; otherwise, the Shuffle might fall off.

Recharging Your Shuffle

The Shuffle doesn't come with a wall plug. Connect it to your computer to recharge it, although you want to make sure the computer is on.

It gets 80 percent charged after 2 hours and fully charged after 4 hours.

The Least You Need to Know

- The Shuffle doesn't use the Apple Touch Wheel.
- You can't select your music, but you can tell it what collection to gather music from.
- Plug the Shuffle directly into your computer—no wires.
- Green means sizable power, amber means low power, red means almost no power.
- Shuffles hold approximately 120–240 songs.

iPod Photo

In This Chapter

- Differences between Photo and other iPods
- How to transfer photos
- Maximizing your Photo's space

The iPod Photo is the biggest of the series, perfect for folks with large music libraries or a digital camera. This chapter explains how to make the best use of the iPod Photo's power.

It's Like a Fancy iPod

The iPod Photo is almost exactly like the Original and Mini, except for a few key differences:

- It has a full-color screen.
- It can carry and display your pictures.
- The smallest Photo can carry more music than the largest Original.

> ♫ **Music to Your Ears** _____
>
> The average home computer today has about 60 GB of space, the same amount of memory in your little iPod Photo.

Music transfer, playlists, and other functions are identical to the Original and Mini/Nano models, so you can read Chapter 5 to get the basics. This chapter just goes over the functions unique to the iPod Photo.

Menu Options

The iPod Photo's top menu has two additions: Photo and Shuffle Songs. Photo opens up a whole list of digital photography options discussed later in this chapter. Shuffle Songs automatically randomizes your next listening session (like the iPod Shuffle and later-generation iPod Originals). Just highlight Shuffle Songs and press the Select button.

More Music, Decent Battery Life

You can carry 50 percent more music in the 30 GB, smaller iPod Photo than the 20 GB, larger iPod Original. The larger iPod Photo packs 60 GB and can carry 3 times the music of the Original, roughly 15,000 songs.

The iPod Photo battery lasts 15 hours, about 3 hours longer than the Original and Mini models. Conversely, the Shuffle lasts 18 hours.

Transferring Photos to iPod

Use your favorite digital camera to transfer your photos to your computer. Alternatively, you can get your standard film developed digitally and put on a CD—most drugstores and convenience stores can process it for you. Then you can transfer it to your iPod for easy travel.

Heads Up

You can also transfer photos from camera to iPod using the optional iPod Camera Connector, but the instructions are camera-specific, and not all brands are compatible. Visit www.apple.com/support/ipod/photos for more information.

After you have your photos on your computer, start up iTunes and connect your iPod Photo to the computer. Click the small iPod icon in the lower-left corner, right next to the Equalizer button. Doing so pops up the iPod Options screen.

Finding Your Computer Photos

Click the Photo tab to display a list of options. The first, Synchronize photos from:, tells the iPod from where to get your photos.

You have three choices:

- Photoshop Album or iPhoto
- Picture Folder
- Choose Folder

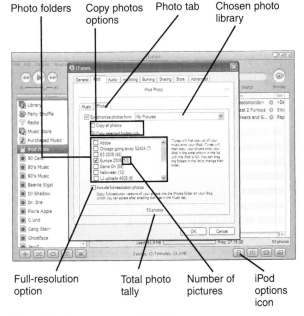

Importing pictures to your iPod Photo.

If you use a PC and Adobe Photoshop Album 1.0/Photoshop Elements 3.0 or later to organize your photos, your computer would have created groups of pictures called Photoshop Albums. The Photoshop Album choice is best for Adobe users.

If you are a Mac user and you use iPhoto 4.0.3 or later, your computer would have created a special iPhoto group of pictures. The iPhoto choice is best for iPhoto users.

If you use none of the above programs, your program probably put your pictures into a generic picture file called Pictures or My Pictures. This will be choice number two on the Synchronize photos from: list.

Finally, if your photo files don't appear on either list, select Choose Folder, and you can tell iTunes where your pictures are located on your computer.

Copying Photos

After you find your photo folders, you can tell iTunes to either copy all the photos from the folders to your iPod or take only specified folders. This option displays right below the Synchronize photos from: option.

Crossed Wires

Be careful with choosing Copy all photos. The process could take more than an hour.

If you decide to Copy all photos, the iPod Photo takes as many pictures as it has room for.

When you pick Copy selected folders only, iTunes gives you a list of the different sets of pictures within your album, their name, and how many pictures are in each. You can then check off which ones you want to include by clicking the box on the left. A tally of the total number of pictures you have selected displays at the bottom of the Options screen.

iTunes fills your iPod with the pictures in order until it finishes or runs out of space. You can drag the folders around to change the order of priority.

Photo Compression

iTunes automatically compresses your photos before it transfers them to the device to save space. Click the Include full-resolution photos box if you want it to save your photos at regular size. It takes up more memory, but this method gives you an additional full-size copy of your digital pictures.

Click OK. iTunes will begin transferring your photos to the iPod Photo.

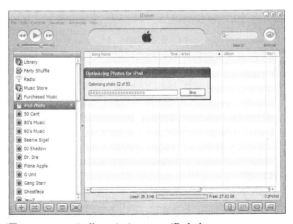

iTunes automatically optimizes your iPod photos.

Viewing Pics

On your iPod, click the Photos option on the top
menu screen. The menu then lists Slideshow
Settings and Photo Library, along with any specific
photo folders you have uploaded to the iPod.

Photo Library vs. Specific Libraries

Photo Library is where you can view all the photos
on your iPod, not just those in a specific folder.
Both the Photo Library and your specific folders
operate the same way.

Navigating Your Collection

The iPod shows small versions of the photos, called
thumbnails, 5×5 across the screen. Turn the Apple
Touch Wheel clockwise or counterclockwise to go
forward or backward through the pictures. When
you find a picture you want to see, press the Select
button. The picture will fill the display screen.

Press the Next/Fast-Forward button to go to the next
picture and Previous/Rewind to go to the previous
one. Moving the Apple Touch Wheel clockwise and
counterclockwise enables you to move forward or
backward through the pictures quickly. Pressing
Menu brings you back to the picture select screen.

Slideshows

Your iPod Photo can also do an impromptu slideshow featuring all your photos or pictures from a
specific folder.

Watching on Your iPod

Find the photo you want the slideshow to begin with and press the Select button so that the photo fills the display screen. Then press the Play/Pause or Select buttons again to begin a slideshow.

Watching on an External Device

You can also look at your slideshow on a TV, monitor, or projector using the optional iPod AV cable. The three-prong AV wire has one video and two audio plugs on one end, which connect to your output device, and a plug on the other end that connects to the Dock Connector port at the bottom of your iPod. It is sold separately for less than $30.

Controls During the Slideshow

Press the Play/Pause button to pause or begin the slideshow. Next/Fast-Forward skips you to the next picture, and Previous/Rewind takes you back. The Menu button returns you to the picture select screen.

Crossed Wires

The iPod Photo battery life lasts less than 5 hours while doing a slideshow with music. Be sure to plug it in during your presentation.

Different Slideshow Settings

To access the slideshow settings, press Menu until you reach the top menu. Then select Photos, and then Slideshow Settings.

Slideshow Options

Time Per Slide	Set the gap from 2 to 20 seconds, or to manual.
Music	Select a playlist for slideshow background music.
Repeat	Switch on or off.
Shuffle Photos	Randomize the pictures during the slideshow.
Transitions	Switch screen wipes on or off.
TV Out	Tell iPod to ask if you want TV output.
TV Signal	Set to NTSC (generally America) or PAL (Europe).

TV Out can be set to On, Off, or Ask. On assumes that you want your slideshow shown on a TV if connected. Off assumes you do not. Ask prompts you every time a new slideshow begins and asks whether you want it displayed on the connected TV.

Formatting Pictures

The format you save your digital pictures in isn't too much of an issue with the iPod Photo because it is compatible with all the major picture formats, including the following:

- JPEG
- BMP
- GIF
- TIFF
- PSD
- PNG

However, watch your picture size—the larger your pictures, the more memory they take up and, consequently, the fewer pictures (and music) you can carry on your iPod Photo.

To conserve space, pictures should generally be no bigger than 1200×800 (horizontally) and take up less than 500 K of memory.

The Least You Need to Know

- iPod Photos carry approximately 7,500–15,000 songs.
- They can carry virtually any digital photo format.
- iTunes automatically compresses your photos to save space.
- Show your photos on TV using the optional AV wire.

Accessorize!

In This Chapter

- Items included with your iPod
- Speakers, carrying cases, and other extra accessories
- Fun things to buy

The iPod is one of the most customizable music devices out there. It comes packed with everything you need, but there are dozens of accessories by Apple and other companies that will help you tailor your iPod to your needs. In this chapter, you learn how to maximize your iPod experience.

What Your iPod Comes With

All iPods come with the basic necessities that vary based on the model.

iPod Standard Accessories

Model	Comes With
Original	Earbud headphones, AC adaptor, FireWire cable, USB 2.0 cable, wall plug
Mini	Earbud headphones, belt clip, USB 2.0 cable, wall plug
Shuffle	Earbud headphones, lanyard, USB cap, wall plug
Photo	Earbud headphones, AC adapter, USB 2.0 cable, wall plug

Special iPods

Apple and other companies sometimes produce special limited-edition iPods. For instance, the band U2 sponsored an Original iPod in 2004. It featured red-and-black casing instead of the usual white and a $50 discount off a U2 Best-Of collection available through the Apple Music Store.

Stuff to Buy

Both Apple and third-party vendors such as Bose and Belkin offer plenty of accessories.

Heads Up

The Apple iPod website (www.apple.com/ipod) is regularly updated with the newest iPod accessories.

Headphones

The basic iPod headphones are earbuds, tiny round plugs that stick in your ear. If you aren't a fan of earbuds, just pick up another basic set of headphones— you can use the same headphones for your iPod that are used for other portable music devices such as tape and CD players. Apple also sells alternative earphones. Literally, you have hundreds of options from which to choose.

Speakers

Bose, JBL, and other companies have special speakers especially made for the iPod. Most are structured like a flat screen with a space in the middle to plug in your iPod securely. One particularly cool setup offered by Apple and other companies uses a wireless signal to connect your iPod with speakers around the house.

Traditional portable music device speakers that just plug into the headphones jack also work with the iPod.

Travel Accessories

Travelers take note: Apple's got you covered. Some of the most useful products are the Apple World Travel Adapter Kit, a smattering of outlet plugs that enable you to recharge from nearly anywhere on the planet, and the Monster iCase Travel Pack, a handy case that keeps your iPod accessories organized.

There are also the standard car accessories, such as the Sony Car Cassette Adapter, which enables you to listen to your iPod through a tape deck.

Engravings

Buying your iPod directly from Apple online gives you the option of having it engraved. It is usually free, though it can add 4 to 6 weeks to your delivery time.

Recharge Accessories

Aside from wall plugs, recharging on the road can be done using one of the car recharging accessories, such as the Belkin Auto Charger, that fits in your cigarette lighter. Apple itself provides the iPod Dock, a small, upright stand that charges your iPod and provides an audio jack so that you can still listen during the recharge.

Covers and Cases

Apple and several third-party companies have sleeves that protect your iPod from wear and tear. Be aware that cases add bulk to your iPod, so your iPod Mini with case may be the size of an Original.

Running Accessories

Carrying cases from third-party companies such as Marware come with adjustable armbands for easy jogging.

Heads Up _____

The iPod Shuffle, despite its wearable lanyard and light weight, also has armbands and other running accessories available.

Fun Stuff

There is no shortage of fun (and funny) accessories out there for your iPod. For instance, the Cellulounger is a cute miniature lounge chair to rest your iPod in when not in use. A fun item from Apple itself is the iPod Sock—a knit slipcover that keeps your iPod snug.

The Least You Need to Know

- All iPods come with earbud headphones and an iTunes software CD.
- Several companies sell iPod home speakers.
- Most accessories are not compatible with Shuffle.
- Buy a cover for your iPod as soon as possible.

Chapter 9

Advanced iPod Techniques

In This Chapter

- How to transfer files
- Having fun with iPod extras
- Tailoring your iPod experience

You can take your iPod straight out of the box and play your tunes, but the little guy also packs a lot of cool functions. In this chapter, you learn how to play games, keep organized, and even turn your iPod into a portable hard drive.

Backing Up Your Music Collection

It's crucial that you back up your music collection to CDs—you don't want to lose your whole stash because of a lost laptop or a malfunctioning computer. iTunes makes it a straightforward process.

The first time you back up your music collection, you want to copy the whole library. After your initial backup, you should then only back up the new music you've gotten since your last backup.

You can back up your library on burnable CDs or DVDs. Although it might seem counterintuitive to *physically* back up your music on the very same medium you copied your music from, your whole music collection will now fit on a few CDs as opposed to being spread across hundreds.

Heads Up

CDs are cheap, but you will need many to store your music collection. DVDs cost more and require a DVD burner, but you will need fewer discs.

Your Whole Library

Backing up your whole music library can take a few hours, but you only need to check on your computer to change discs or see its current progress.

To back up your entire music library, follow these steps:

1. Insert the CD or DVD into your computer.
2. Click the Library icon in the left column.
3. Press the Browse (the eye) button in the upper-right corner.
4. Click All under the Genre, Artist and Album column.
5. Pull down the Edit menu on PC or iTunes menu on Mac at the very top and click Select All.

6. Pull down the File menu at the very top and click New Playlist From Selection.

7. Name the backup by date, such as Backup January 2006.

8. Burn your CD or DVD as indicated in the following "Burning Your Music" section.

Your music collection will probably require more than one CD or DVD. iTunes lets you know when the current disc is full and gives you the option to continue the backup on another disc until the backup is complete.

Crossed Wires

Note the date when you do your full backup. If you don't, you'll have to guess the last backup date when you ask iTunes to back up only your newest songs.

Only Your New Music

Luckily you don't have to back up your whole music library every time. iTunes lets you make copies of just the new music you've gotten since your last backup. However, it's crucial to know when your last backup was to do this efficiently.

To back up your most recent music additions, follow these steps:

1. Pull down the File menu at the very top and click New Smart Playlist.

2. Move the first option to Date Added.

3. Move the second option to Is after.

4. Type in your last backup date in the last box.

5. Name the backup by date, such as Backup January 2006.

6. Burn your CD or DVD as indicated in the following "Burning Your Music" section.

You should back up your music at least every two to three months, more often if you copy or download music frequently.

Burning Your Music

You actually burn your backup CDs and DVDs differently than traditional CDs. iTunes compresses them for you so that you can fit more onto one disc, but you have to tell it first. After you set the format, you can burn it just like a playlist.

Heads Up

Review Chapter 2 to get a refresher on how to do basic and smart playlists.

To format your special backup disc(s), follow these steps:

1. Pull down the Edit menu on PC or iTunes menu on Mac at the very top and click Preferences.

2. Click the Burning tab.
3. Under disc format, select Data CD or DVD.
4. Click OK.
5. Burn your backup playlist as you would any other playlist.
6. Pull down the Edit menu on PC or iTunes menu on Mac at the very top and click Preferences.
7. Click the Burning tab.
8. Under disc format, select Audio CD.
9. Click OK.

Crossed Wires _____

Be sure to change the disc format to Data CD or DVD when backing up, and then to Audio CD when you're done. Otherwise your CDs won't be backed up or burned correctly!

iPod as Portable Hard Drive

You can also use the iPod to transfer files like a portable *hard drive*. Here's how.

iTerms

The **hard drive** is the main area where a computer stores information. The iPod uses its hard drive to hold your music, photos, and other files.

Turning On the Hard Drive

Connect your iPod to the computer and start iTunes. Make sure your iPod icon is highlighted. Click the Options button in the lower-right corner. The Options menu will pop up.

Click the iPod tab at the top of the Options box. Then select Enable disk use.

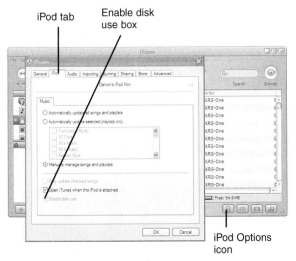

Go to the Options screen to enable your iPod hard drive.

Transferring Files

You can now use your iPod to carry files just like any other portable storage device. You move files through the computer directory, not iTunes. If you have a file you want to take with you or want to back up, you …

1. Find the IPOD hard drive listing.
2. Drag the file you need into the folder.

On Macs, the IPOD hard drive appears on your desktop. On PCs, it is usually designated as the E: drive (C: is usually your hard drive, D: your CD or DVD drive) and can be accessed through the My Computer icon.

When you want to access the file later, connect the iPod again, find the hard drive as you did before, and drag your file back onto your computer desktop or respective computer folder.

Alternatively, you can have iTunes automatically update your playlists. Go to the top of the screen, click on the Edit menu, and then select Preferences. Click on the iPod tab, then the Music tab to see your automatic music update options.

For instance, suppose you have a traveling playlist called CarMix1. You put the playlist on your iPod, but later you find two more songs that would also go well on your mix, so you add them to your iTunes playlist. If you check Automatically update all songs and playlists, iTunes adds the two new songs to your iPod the next time you connect it.

Next to the Music tab you'll see the Podcast tab. Click on it to choose between Podcast automatic update options. Like the Music tab, you can Automatically update all podcasts, Automatically update selected podcasts only, or not automatically update any. If you do decide to automatically update, the small update bar at the bottom allows you to choose to update only the most recent episodes. You can read more about podcasting in Chapter 10.

Other iPod Options

Aside from the hard drive (which is listed under the iPod tab), plenty of other secrets are hidden within the Options menu.

You can access these as you accessed the hard drive menu. Connect your iPod to the computer and start iTunes. Make sure your iPod icon is highlighted. Click the Options button in the lower-right corner. The Options menu will pop up.

Heads Up _____

These options are also available by selecting Preferences under the Edit menu at the top of iTunes.

Click the respective tab at the top of the Options menu.

General

This is the first tab of the iTunes Options menu. The top selections affect your text size and the number of icons shown in your left column. The middle selections change the way you browse for new music. The bottom selections determine what happens when you insert a new music CD.

General tab   Display options

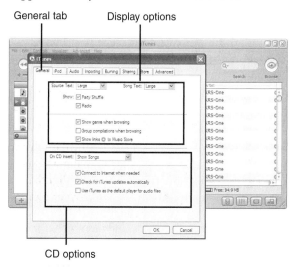

CD options

The General Options screen controls the iTunes display.

iPod

As described earlier, this is where you can select automatic song updating so you won't have to drag new music or podcasts onto the iPod yourself.

Podcasts

From here you can control your podcast frequency. Read more about podcasting in Chapter 10.

The first option, Check for new episodes, allows you to check for new podcast content every hour, day, or week. You can also switch it to manual.

The second option, When new episodes are available, lets you automatically download all the new episodes or just download the latest one. For instance, if you're out of town and miss the last four podcasts of your favorite program, iTunes can either download all four for you or just the latest episode. You can also tell it to not download anything automatically.

With the third option, Keep, you determine how many back episodes you want iTunes to store for you. This ranges from all episodes to none.

Finally, clicking on the iPod Preferences button will refer you back to the previous tab, iPod.

Audio

Here are the cool audio effects you can turn on.

Crossfade playback starts the next song a few seconds before the preceding song is over, overlapping the two songs and making it sound like a continuous mix.

Heads Up

You can crossfade, or overlap, up to 12 seconds of back-to-back songs.

Sound Enhancer makes your songs crisper and clearer. Sound Check evens out the music so that all your songs are the same volume (great when you're listening on headphones).

The bottom options tweak your remote speaker controls if you've got 'em.

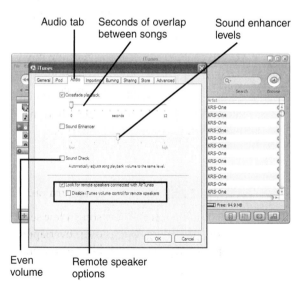

Audio tab   Seconds of overlap   Sound enhancer
                 between songs   levels

Even   Remote speaker
volume   options

Tweak the sound on the Audio Options tab.

Importing

The Importing tab has your preferences when you copy CDs to iTunes.

Import Using enables you to choose the format you record the CD music in:

- AAC Encoder
- AIFF Encoder
- Apple Lossless Encoder
- MP3 Encoder
- WAV Encoder

AAC is the default iTunes and iPod format. MP3 is the industry standard for most other players, so recording in MP3 format is worth considering if you're using other portable music players. Otherwise, AAC is the best choice.

Setting determines the amount of memory used to record your songs—the higher the number, the higher the quality. 128 kbps is considered high quality, but the lower options available, like 64 kbps, take up less space on your computer (but at the loss of some clarity). The higher quality your earphones or speakers, the more you'll notice this quality loss.

Try recording a CD at a lower quality. If you can't tell the difference, use the Low Quality setting.

The remaining Importing list is pretty inconsequential except for Use error correction when reading Audio CDs, which is handy when the CD you're trying to import is scratchy.

Crossed Wires

The WAV format is the least practical for iTunes. This format creates larger music files, which means you can carry less music in iTunes and particularly on your iPod.

Importing tab   Music format choices

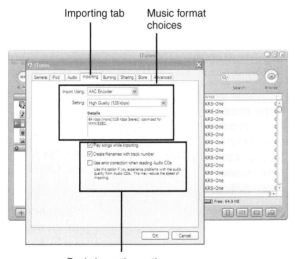

Basic importing options

Set the music quality on the Importing screen.

Burning

This is a great place to get information on your CD burner.

Aside from CD/DVD information, choose your CD burn speed, CD format, and space between songs, if any.

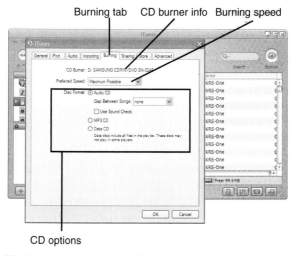

Heads Up

A natural pause occurs between songs on a CD, so you usually don't have to exercise this option.

Burning tab   CD burner info   Burning speed

CD options

The Burning tab gives you CD burner information.

Sharing

If you are on a network or have multiple computer users, the Sharing tab lets you decide which songs or playlists you want to share with other users. To share, click the Share my music box, and then either Share entire library or Share selected playlists, and choose which specific mixes you want to share.

Click the Require password box and type in a
secret password if you want added security.

Sharing music   Sharing tab   Selected
choices   playlists

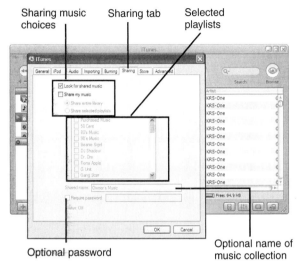

Optional password   Optional name of
music collection

Make your music available to other computer users.

Store

Select your Apple Music Store preferences here,
such as 1-Click (immediate) purchasing versus
Shopping Cart browsing.

Store options for when you go iTunes shopping.

Heads Up

Shopping Cart browsing is best if you have multiple Apple Music Store accounts in your household.

Advanced

Here are all the techie details that may come in handy.

iTunes Advanced Options Tab

Type	What It Does
Folder Location	Where music is being saved on the hard drive
Buffer Size	Space made for temporary music download
Shuffle by	Mix it up by song or whole albums

The remaining options help you organize your music and your desktop.

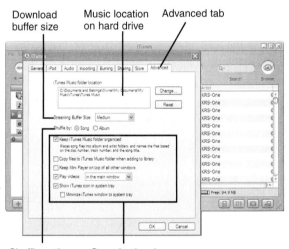

The Advanced tab has all the nitty-gritty details.

Extras

The iPod is chock full of extras that you may or may not end up using. Unfortunately, because it has no screen, these extras aren't available on the iPod Shuffle.

Clock

You have three options under the Clock menu:

- Alarm Clock
- Sleep Timer
- Date & Time

Alarm Clock enables you to set the iPod to ring and flash its screen at a particular time. You choose the time under the Time menu option. Under the Sound option you select the preferred alarm call: a basic beep or a music selection from a particular playlist.

Crossed Wires

Be sure your iPod is charged before using the Alarm Clock function! You don't want it to shut off before it wakes you up.

Sleep Timer shuts down your iPod at a particular interval, anywhere from 15 minutes to 120 minutes from when you select this option.

Finally, the Date & Time option is identical to the one in the Settings menu.

Contacts

All computers can transfer contact info, but Mac users have it a little easier than PC users.

For Mac users, follow these steps:

1. Open the iSync program.
2. Go to menu and highlight Devices, and then Add Device.
3. Highlight iPod and click the Sync Now option.

Heads Up _____

The Apple iSync program can be used not only to synchronize your Mac and your iPod, but also your Mac to other Apple devices.

For PC users, follow these steps:

1. Open your e-mail/contacts program.
2. Go to the Contacts list.
3. Then go to My Computer.
4. Find and double-click the IPOD hard drive listing (usually the E: drive).
5. Double-click the IPOD Contacts folder.

6. Drag the contacts you need from the e-mail program to the IPOD Contacts folder.

Go to the Contacts menu, under your iPod Extras menu, to see your contacts.

Contact information from the PC works best with Eudora, Microsoft Outlook or Entourage, and Palm Desktop.

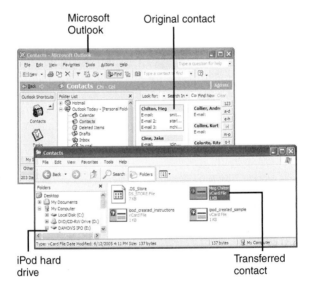

Manually transferring contacts on the PC.

Crossed Wires

The iPod only reads contacts in the vCard format. Open the contact and Save As vCard if necessary.

Calendar

Unfortunately, you can only save your calendar on your iPod if you're using a Mac. To save your calendar on your iPod, open any calendar program that uses the iCalendar (.ICS) or vCal (.VCS) format.

1. Open up your computer directory.
2. Find the IPOD hard drive listing.
3. Double-click it to find the Calendar folder.
4. Drag your iCalendar or vCal calendar into the folder.

You can now go to the Calendar menu, under your iPod Extras menu, to look at your calendar.

Notes

To save text notes on your iPod, open your favorite word processing program, write your notes, and save them as a .TXT (text) file.

1. Open up your computer directory.
2. Find the IPOD hard drive listing.
3. Double-click it to find the Notes folder.
4. Drag your note into the folder.

You can now go to the Notes menu, under your iPod Extras menu, and read your list.

Unfortunately, after you have finished with a note, you can't delete it directly from your iPod. You have to do it through your computer.

To delete a note from your iPod, follow these steps:

1. Reconnect your iPod.
2. Open your computer directory.
3. Find the IPOD hard drive listing.
4. Double-click it to find the Notes folder.
5. Delete your unwanted note.

Games

The games on your iPod vary per model, but usually include the following titles:

- **Brick.** Similar to the classic Atari game Breakout, you use a bat to bounce a ball against a pile of bricks. The Apple Touch Wheel moves the bat left and right.

- **Music Quiz.** Like the game show *Name That Tune*, the iPod plays songs from your music library and tests you on how quickly you can guess the song. You're given a choice between four song titles and given a score based on your speed and accuracy.

- **Solitaire.** The traditional card game translates well to your iPod. The visuals are fine on the Original and Mini, but the color iPod Photo version looks great.

The Least You Need to Know

- Turn on your iPod hard drive on the Options menu: "Enable disk use."

- AAC is the default iTunes music format, but MP3 is the general standard.

- Hold contacts, calendars, and notes on your iPod.

- Mac users can automatically sync their iPod with their computer.

- Back up your music on CD or DVD every month or so.

On the Air

In This Chapter

- What is podcasting?
- How to find podcast programming
- Getting it on your iPod

iPods already let you be your own DJ, but with podcasting, you can become your own radio news director. Through iTunes you have access to hundreds of different (and free) prerecorded broadcasts on topics ranging from basketball to basket weaving.

What the Heck Is Podcasting?

Podcasting is a way to listen to your own personal set of radio programs on your computer or on your iPod. Through iTunes, prerecorded shows are automatically downloaded to your computer as they arrive. You can then transfer your favorite shows to your iPod and listen to them on the road. (If you have a TiVo or other digital video recorder, this is very similar to how you record every episode of your favorite TV shows.)

Getting the Right Software

In summer 2005 Apple put podcasting software right into your iTunes list, the second item in the left column between Library and Party Shuffle. Click on the Podcasts icon to get started.

> ## Heads Up
>
> To podcast, you need iTunes version 4.9 or later. You can download the latest version of iTunes at www.apple.com/ipod/download.

Getting Started with Podcasting

After clicking on the Podcasts icon you'll be taken to your podcast listings. If it's your first time, it should be empty.

Four options line the bottom of your listings: the Podcast Directory and Report a Concern arrows, and the Unsubscribe and Settings buttons.

Click on the Report a Concern arrow to contact Apple about a problem. The Settings button will take you to the Podcast Preferences as explained in Chapter 9.

The most important options are the Podcast Directory arrow and the Unsubscribe button.

Podcast Directory

Clicking on the Podcast Directory arrow will take you to the music store. Don't worry—virtually all podcasts are free (at least for the near future!). Apple has organized podcasts within the Apple Music Store for organizational purposes.

Here you'll find little ads for podcasts, ranging from ESPN basketball coverage to CBS Marketwatch financial news. There are also plenty of independent news and music programs available.

Along the right side you'll find the top 10 most popular podcast downloads. At the end of this list you can click on the Top 100 Podcasts arrow to see more options.

In the lower-left side you'll find Categories ranging from Arts & Entertainment to Travel. Click on a category or one of the flashing advertisements to see the prerecorded programs available today.

♫ Music to Your Ears

> Prerecorded radio shows may sound less than ideal, but many "live" radio shows on major stations such as National Public Radio (NPR) or the British Broadcasting Corporation (BBC) are preprogrammed, too.

Clicking a front-page ad will give you a show summary along the top half of the screen. The left section gives the number of episodes, category (such as

News or Sports), and language. The right section gives a brief podcast description and a link to the program website. The current programs available are listed on the bottom half like songs, showing the program name, time, artist (a.k.a. Host), release date, brief program description, and price, which is free.

Clicking a front-page category will take you to a much broader listing section where you can find shows based on genre, category, and subcategory. Define what you want to narrow your search.

For instance, let's say I want to subscribe to a program that will tell me about all the latest XBox video game system news. I would make sure the Genre, which is always Podcast, is highlighted. Then I would make sure that the Category is set to Arts & Entertainment. Finally, I would set the Subcategory to Games.

iTunes would then give me a listing of the related shows, some of which cover the XBox game system. The listing is similar to the Apple Music Store song listings. The shows are organized by Name, Time, Artist (a.k.a. Host), and other factors. The final listing is price, which is free.

If a program interests you, click the button next to the price, which will read "Get Episode" or "Subscribe." iTunes will then download the latest episode to your previously empty podcast listing section. You can now listen to it whenever you like, using your song controls to pause, play, fast-forward, or rewind the program.

Crossed Wires

Some podcasts say "Get Episode," which means you can download just the episodes you want without commitment. However, those that say "Subscribe Only" require you to cancel your subscription to stop getting regular episodes in the future.

Unsubscribe

If you pressed the "Subscribe" button for your podcast, you can expect more episodes to be downloaded for you in the future. The frequency is determined by when the next episode is available as well as your own download frequencies set under the Podcast Preferences menu. You can visit this menu by pressing the Settings button at the bottom of the screen.

Tired of subscribing to a program? Highlight the program and press the Unsubscribe button, which is located to the left of the Settings button. The "Subscribe" option will appear next to the podcast program name so you can re-subscribe if you change your mind later.

You can delete programs by highlighting them and pressing the Delete key on the keyboard.

Crossed Wires _____

You don't pay for subscriptions. Getting a subscription just means you want to know when new show episodes come.

Transferring to iPod

To listen to a podcast on your iPod, put your mouse cursor over the program name, and hold down the mouse button and drag it into your iPod icon just as you would a song.

Alternatively, you can have iTunes automatically update the device with your latest podcast downloads. Do this by clicking the Settings button in the lower-right corner, clicking the iPod tab, and then clicking the Podcast tab.

Here you can Automatically update all podcasts, Automatically update selected podcasts only, or not automatically update any.

- Automatically update all podcasts transfers the latest podcasts to your iPod every time you plug it into your computer.

- Automatically update selected podcasts only does the same, except you must tell iTunes which podcasts to automatically update. iTunes gives you a list of your current podcasts. Click on the ones you would like automatically updated.

A small update bar at the bottom allows you to choose to update your iPod with only the most recent episodes.

Adding Programs on Your Own

There are perhaps thousands of podcast shows online with many more being started every day. Because of the sheer number of shows out there, Apple does not have all of them available through the Apple Music Store. However, if you are exploring on the Internet and hear about a show you want to subscribe to that isn't available through Apple, you can add it to your iTunes yourself.

First, find out the web address of the podcast show. It will look similar to a traditional website address.

Next, you'll want to copy that podcast address. Once you do that, go to the Advanced menu at the top of your iTunes screen and select Subscribe to Podcast. Paste the address in the box and click the OK button. iTunes will now treat your new show the same way it would one added through the Apple Music Store.

The Least You Need to Know

- Podcasting is listening to preprogrammed radio shows.
- You need iTunes version 4.9 or later to podcast.
- Subscribe to have iTunes periodically download the latest episodes.
- Podcast listings are at the Apple Music Store.

Keeping Your iPod Up and Runnin'

In This Chapter

- iPod maintenance
- Efficient backlight use
- Troubleshooting

Taking care of your little iPod is important, especially with its high-tech insides carrying your music and photos. In this chapter, you'll find tips on keeping your iPod in good condition, as well as a trouble-shooting checklist to help with any problems you may have.

Warranty Information

All iPods have a limited one-year warranty and single-incident telephone support for the first 90 days of purchase—meaning that you can call Apple once for free support.

It's worthwhile to look into AppleCare Protection Plan for iPod. Currently $59, AppleCare extends support and service to two years and insures your accessories and software. It can be purchased from Apple when you buy your iPod.

It also includes

- Toll-free number for tech support
- Replacement parts approved by Apple
- Transfer of the insurance plan between owners

Tips for iPod Care

The iPod has a tough outer shell, but you're still carrying around a small computer with sensitive equipment. You can prolong the life of your iPod in several ways.

Crossed Wires _____

It's almost inevitable that your soft earphone covers will fall off and disappear during regular iPod use. Apple includes an extra set with your iPod, and more can be ordered online through the Apple website.

Buy a Case

iPod Shuffles are small and durable, but the other iPods have a vulnerable screen. To avoid scratches and cracks, get some type of case immediately after purchase. See Chapter 8 for accessories for some suggestions.

Avoid Extreme Temperatures and Water

Apple recommends running your iPod only when it is between 32 and 95 degrees Fahrenheit (0 to 35 degrees Celsius), which may not always be possible in your climate, but still something to keep in mind.

When not being used, your iPod should be kept in a place between –4 and 113 degrees Fahrenheit (–20 to 45 degrees Celsius)—a much easier range to follow. Remember this if you decide to take your iPod to Siberia or the Sahara.

Direct sunlight can discolor (not to mention bake) your little iPod, as well as your accessories. Your power adapter is particularly sensitive.

Also, because it's an electronic device, keep it from getting wet at all costs. Third-party companies offer iPod waterproof cases, but it would be best to avoid water without them.

Clean Carefully

Use a slightly damp, soft cloth to clean your equipment, preferably one that is lint- and static-free. Don't leave it connected to the computer or wall outlet when you're cleaning.

Apple suggests avoiding aerosol sprays, solvents, alcohol, or abrasives. They aren't really necessary.

Don't Use Alternative Wall Plugs

Alternative headphones are fine; if you happen to misplace your iPod wall plug, however, don't go to the corner electronics store for a replacement unless they are an authorized Apple dealer. A bad wall plug could fry your iPod. It's best to contact Apple itself or visit the Apple website (www.apple.com) and order your replacement parts online.

Backlight vs. Battery Life

Using the backlight continuously on any of the models will put a serious drain on the battery, cutting the charge almost in half.

If you like using the backlight, use the Backlight Timer, under the Settings menu, to have the light go off after a set period of time.

Resetting Your iPod

If your iPod is "frozen" or acting strange, you may just need to reset it. Here's how.

Crossed Wires

Resetting and restoring your iPod aren't the same! Resetting is basically turning it on and off. Restoring is erasing your iPod's memory (a.k.a. your songs and settings).

Resetting iPod Mini/Nanos, Photos, and Later-Generation Originals

To reset iPod Mini/Nanos, Photos, and later-generation Originals ...

1. Turn the Hold switch on and off.
2. Hold the Menu and Select buttons for 10 seconds.
3. Connect it to a wall outlet if it doesn't reset.

Resetting All Other Original iPods

To reset all other Original iPods ...

1. Turn the Hold switch on and off.
2. Hold the Play/Pause and Menu buttons for 10 seconds.
3. Connect it to a wall outlet if it doesn't reset.

Update vs. Restore

Like Windows and other computer programs, Apple routinely corrects errors in the iPod software. You are given a notice in iTunes when updates are available.

On the other hand, restoring erases your iPod—that is, restoring it to "factory condition." It will eliminate all your music and settings, so this is definitely a last resort.

Restoring on Macs

To restore on a Mac ...

1. Connect your iPod to the computer.
2. Close iTunes.
3. Click on your Applications folder.
4. Click on the Utilities folder.
5. Click on the padlock button.
6. Click the Restore button.
7. Follow onscreen instructions.

Restoring on Windows

To restore on Windows ...

1. Click on the Start icon.
2. Click on All Programs.
3. Click on iPod.
4. Click on iPod Updater.
5. Follow the onscreen instructions to Restore.

Icons

Your iPod screen usually will show nothing more than the current menu or the song now playing. Other times, the machine will let you know what's happening by showing icons. Here's what they mean.

Apple Logo

Your iPod is loading. This icon shows when you load up your iPod or are shutting it down. It usually takes a few seconds to load.

Battery with Exclamation Point

You need to recharge your iPod.

CD with Small Magnifying Glass

Your iPod is trying to correct an error within itself. This is automatic, and the process can take up to 20 minutes. Once it's done examining itself, it will give you a diagnosis:

- Checkmark—Everything's OK.
- Exclamation point—Your iPod is corrupted. Call an Apple specialist and arrange to get repairs.
- Right arrow—Your iPod found some internal problems, but it was able to correct them. You should restore your iPod after you get this icon.
- X symbol—You cancelled the diagnostic by holding down the center button. It will continue the next time you turn the iPod on.

Do Not Disconnect

Your iPod is connected to a computer. Press the Eject iPod button on your iTunes before you unplug it.

Folder with an Exclamation Point

This pops up only if you're using a PC with your iPod (not a Mac). It could mean several things:

- The battery needs to be charged.
- Your iPod software needs to be updated—connect to a computer and download the latest Apple update.
- Your iPod may have simply locked up—reset your iPod.
- It may need repairs—contact Apple.

Little iPod Picture with Sad Face

Your iPod needs repairs. Contact Apple.

Power Adapter Drawing

Your iPod sometimes needs to reset itself after a new update. Connect it to a plug with your wall adapter to reset it.

Troubleshooting

The iPod has its quirks just like any other computer device. Here are some troubleshooting suggestions.

No Response from the Computer

If your computer isn't responding when you hook up your iPod, you might have forgotten to install the iTunes program from the included CD.

If you're all installed, check the iPod wire and make sure it's secure to the bottom of the device. Remember that you need to press the small tabs on the side of the wire's flat end to put it in the iPod, and then release the tabs to make it secure. Your computer makes a ding noise when a connection is made.

In fact, if you hear the ding noise but see no change on your computer, give it a second—it can take time for the computer to upload iTunes and the iPod information.

Worst-case scenario: turn off your computer, then your iPod, turn on your computer, and then reconnect your iPod.

No Music Coming from iPod

If there's no music coming from your iPod, oftentimes it's from leaving the Hold switch on—turn it to the Off position, and you can control the device again. Double-check that your headphones are all the way in, too, and that your volume is high enough.

The iPod has occasional "hiccups" that pause it between songs, which may be why things got quiet.

Worst-case scenario: shut iPod down by holding Play/Pause, charge it up, and then restart it.

iPod Isn't Responding to Buttons

If your iPod isn't responding to buttons, the Hold switch may be the culprit—make sure it isn't in the On position.

Every so often Apple has iTunes/iPod updates that it'll give you a notice about when you get online. Make sure you download the updates when they are recommended, because the problem with your iPod may be software-related.

Worst-case scenario: let the battery completely run down, charge it up, and then restart it.

The Least You Need to Know

- If your iPod is acting strange, disconnect (or reconnect) it to the computer.
- Except for headphones, generally avoid third-party replacement parts.
- Don't get it wet.
- Stay away from extreme hot and cold temperatures.

Important Websites

Using the Internet is essential to getting the best out of your iPod. In this appendix, you'll find websites that will help you get replacement parts, new software, and tips.

Altec Lansing InMotion

www.alteclansing.com

Altec Lansing's InMotion product line features a slew of iPod accessories. Most are surround-sound speakers that double as docking stations for your iPod, such as the barrel-shaped iM7.

Apple iPod

www.ipod.com

If you need information about your specific iPod, this is the place to start. The Apple website has a great breakdown of the different models and a page dedicated to the accessories made especially for your iPod.

iPod Original

www.apple.com/ipod/color

Information on the iPod Original.

iPod Mini

www.apple.com/ipodmini

Details and web links for the two iPod Mini models.

iPod Shuffle

www.apple.com/ipodshuffle

Info on both versions of the iPod Shuffle.

iPod Photo

www.apple.com/ipodphoto

Overview of the iPod Photos available and related material.

iPod Download Site

www.apple.com/ipod/download

If you have a regular Internet connection, iTunes will tell you when there is a new update to your iPod software. If you happen to miss an update, this is the place to download it from.

Apple iTunes

www.itunes.com

Apple also has an extensive website that can answer your iTunes music questions. They also offer links to the newest music online.

iTunes Software Download

www.apple.com/itunes/download

Download the latest version of iTunes for your Mac or PC here. Handy if you happen to misplace your iTunes CD that comes with the iPod.

iTunes Jukebox Information

www.apple.com/itunes/jukebox.html

Links to iTunes websites and more information on the digital jukebox.

iTunes Software Playlist

www.apple.com/itunes/playlists.html

The website for playlist information and assistance.

Apple Music Store

www.apple.com/itunes/store

Different from the iTunes website, the Apple Music Store site gives information specifically related to purchasing music online. Here you'll also find exclusive iTunes music, like a special remix of a current hit song only available through the Apple Music Store and iTunes.

Apple Products Store

http://store.apple.com

An extensive online store where you can buy all the latest Apple products for your iPod. Mac users can also buy accessories, programs, and even computers.

Belkin

www.belkin.com/iPod

Aside from Apple itself, Belkin has perhaps the largest collection of iPod accessories. Among the products available are remotes, replacement cables, and carrying cases. It also is one of the few companies that have accessories for the Shuffle.

Bose

www.bose.com

Bose has a whole line of products for the iPods. A notable one is the SoundDock Digital Music System, which plugs your iPod into a Bose surround-sound speaker system. The gear available isn't made for the iPod Shuffle.

Cellulounger

www.cellulounger.com

Cellulounger is a quirky, small beach chair that can be used to hold your iPod when not in use.

H2O Audio

www.h2oaudio.com

H2O Audio produces waterproof MP3-player cases, including one especially made for the iPod.

iLounge

www.ipodlounge.com

iLounge is an excellent website to get the latest iPod information, as well as links to other Internet resources.

JBL

www.jbl.com

This music component manufacturer has several different speaker setups for the iPod Original, Mini, and Photo.

Marware

www.marware.com

Marware has carrying cases and other accessories for all the iPods.

Glossary

Crossfade? Podcasting? And what are thumbnails? Terms tend to get complicated whenever you start dealing with electronics. Here is a list of definitions to help you along the way. If you're still trying to grasp any words, it will help to look them up within the actual text to see them in context.

AAC   The iTunes/iPod music format that literally stands for Advanced Audio Coding. It is similar to the popular MP3-music format, but is more advanced and generally has a higher sound quality. Unfortunately, the iPod is one of the few portable music players today that uses the AAC format, so users of multiple portable players would be better off using MP3 format.

Apple Music Store   The "virtual" online music store where you can buy music directly from Apple. Whole albums as well as individual album tracks can be downloaded immediately. To go to the store, you must have iTunes installed, an Internet connection, and a major credit card or Apple Music Store gift certificate.

Apple Touch Wheel   A sensitive, flat joystick that is the only control on the later-generation iPod Original, Mini, and Photo. The cardinal directions have the Menu, Next/Fast-Forward, Play/Pause, and Previous/Rewind buttons, and the Select button is in the center of the wheel. Use your thumb to motion along the wheel clockwise or counter-clockwise to navigate menus.

audiobooks   The digital equivalent of books on tape, popular literature read by famous actors or the authors themselves. The Apple Music Store has a large selection of recent books as well as classics to download for your iPod. Most books take multiple hours to listen to and have files larger than most albums.

autofill   The process where iTunes automatically loads your iPod with random music until full. Autofill is the default action for the iPod Shuffle. Autofill mode is also available for the other iPods. You can Autofill from your entire library or from specific playlists.

AV cable   Literally audio-visual cable. You can purchase the optional iPod AV cable to connect your iPod Photo to a TV or projector for slideshows.

backlight   Bright lighting that makes it easier to see your iPod display. Using the backlight continuously during a whole session can cut your battery charge in half. The Backlight Timer option automatically shuts down your iPod backlight after a predetermined time. Doubles nicely as a flashlight.

backlight timer   A setting that shuts down your iPod backlight after a predetermined time. The Backlight Timer parameters can be changed under the iPod Settings menu. Use the Backlight Timer to conserve iPod energy.

crossfade   A disc jockey term for blending two records together during a music set. The crossfade selection under the iTunes Options menu blends the current song and the next song into a seamless mix. You can set the crossfade blending time to up to 12 seconds.

feed   Another term for a podcast show from the Internet. A feed is a specific iPod radio program. When you Add a Feed, it means you are subscribing to the show.

FireWire cord   An alternative to USB cords. Most computers can use both USB and FireWire cords, but some only accept FireWire connections. You can buy the optional FireWire cord to connect your iPod to the computer.

GB (Gigabyte)   A unit of measurement for computer space. On an iPod, one GB can hold about 240 songs. It takes 1,000 MB (megabytes) to make 1 GB.

hard drive   The main memory area where a computer stores information. The iPod uses its hard drive to hold your music and, with the iPod Photo, your pictures. You can enable your iPod to use its hard drive space to hold more traditional computer files such as documents, personal contact information, and a daily calendar.

headphones port   The small hole atop the iPod where you plug in your headphones. You can also plug in alternative music outlets, such as iPod-compatible speakers.

hold switch   A small tab that prevents any iPod button interference. For instance, if you want to listen to music without accidentally pressing a button, push this tab to the On position.

iSync   A Mac program that automatically synchronizes your different Apple software and products. Use it to coordinate information between your iPod and your Mac. It is not available for the PC.

iTunes   A music jukebox for your computer and the main interface between you and your iPod. Through iTunes you can recharge your iPod, change preferences, and access the Apple Music Store.

lanyard   A rope that comes with your iPod Shuffle. Snap your Shuffle to the plastic connector, and you can hang the iPod around your neck. Make sure the Shuffle is securely fastened to the lanyard.

library   Usually means your whole music collection on iTunes. Libraries are broken down into playlists, specific sets of songs that you determine yourself. It can also mean a group of podcast programs.

MB (Megabyte)   A unit of measurement for computer space. On an iPod, 512 MB can hold about 120 songs. It takes just over 1,000 MB to make 1 GB (gigabyte).

MP3   The popular music format that literally stands for Motion Picture Experts Group Audio Layer 3, named after the coalition that created it. iPod and almost every other portable music player accepts the MP3 format. However, the iPod uses the AAC music format by default, a format not compatible with most other portable music players. Go to the Options screen to change the format.

On-The-Go playlist   An impromptu playlist you create on your iPod, as opposed to a traditional playlist you create within the iTunes program. Add songs by finding songs on your iPod Library and holding the Select button until the title flashes. Your iPod will save them in playlists called On-The-Go 1 and so on.

party shuffle   A continuous random song mix played through iTunes. It will play a shuffled list of songs from your general Library or a specific playlist. The party doesn't stop until you intervene.

podcasting   Downloading "radio" programs for listening on your iPod or in iTunes. Regular, pre-recorded shows are available through the Internet, with new programs arriving every day. iTunes Version 4.9 (or later) automatically downloads the latest episodes to your computer.

playlist   A specific set of songs you have put together in a group. It enables you to collect tunes from your library that fit a certain theme, such as dancing, and listen to them together. iTunes can also create playlists for you, called smart playlists, after you give it the parameters.

remote port   A small hole parallel to the Headphones port that is used for the iPod Remote. The optional remote is positioned on your headphone wire, enabling you to control the iPod without having to use the Apple Touch Wheel.

smart playlist   An iTunes-created playlist based on your criteria. For instance, you can tell iTunes to collect all the Jazz songs featuring Ella Fitzgerald along with Mel Torme. Much faster than doing a playlist manually.

sleep   The iPod temporarily turning off. It automatically goes into sleep mode when it hasn't been used in a matter of minutes (to conserve energy) unless the default settings are changed. The larger iPods can be forced into sleep mode by holding the Play/Pause button for three seconds.

subscriptions   Getting regular updates on a particular "radio" show being podcasted. iTunes version 4.9 or later will let you know when a new episode has arrived. Subscriptions are free.

thumbnail   A small version of a photo. The iPod Photo uses thumbnails so that you can quickly scan a group a photos instead of having to flip through each one.

USB cord   The wire connecting your iPod to your computer. The alternative to a USB cord is a FireWire cord, which is usually sold separately.

vCard   A popular file format for personal contact information. Used by Microsoft Outlook and other e-mail/organizational programs, it is the only contact information format the iPod understands.

WAV   Literally stands for WAVe form audio format, created by Microsoft and IBM. This music format option works well with PCs, but the file sizes are larger than MP3 or AAC, making it a less-desirable choice.

Pull-Down Menus

iTunes uses icons and other visual cues to tell you what's going on. However, sometimes you need to get to the nitty-gritty, and that's what the pull-down menus at the very top of the screen are for. Here is a breakdown of the menu options and their various functions.

File

This is where you find things related to importing and exporting music, as well as playlist and burn options.

New Playlist

The same as pressing the Playlist icon, this pull-down creates a basic playlist for you. See Chapter 2 for more information on playlists.

New Playlist from Selection

The pull-down is the same as pressing the Playlist icon. If you highlight a specific group of songs, iTunes will create a basic playlist starting with these songs. See Chapter 2 for more information on playlists.

New Smart Playlist

iTunes will create a smart playlist for you. With smart playlists, you give iTunes certain parameters with which it makes a playlist with songs that fit that criteria. See Chapter 2 for more information on smart playlists.

Add File to Library

Find specific music files on your computer and tell iTunes to make them accessible through your iTunes library. Handy if you imported music files before you started using iTunes.

Add Folder to Library

Find specific music folders on your computer and tell iTunes to make all the music within the folder accessible through your iTunes library. Handy if you imported music files before you started using iTunes.

Close Window

Close iTunes.

Import

If you are using other digital music programs, you transfer music information to iTunes here.

Export Song List

iTunes creates a text listing of all the songs within the highlighted playlist. Genre, time, and other details are included for each song.

Export Library

iTunes creates a complex website file called XML with information on every song in your library.

Get Info

Tells you details on the currently highlighted song, including composer and year produced. See Chapter 8 for more information on Get Info.

My Rating

Adjust or create a rating (one to five stars) for the highlighted song. See Chapter 2 for more information on rating songs within iTunes.

Edit Smart Playlist

With this you can modify the criteria of the highlighted smart playlist. See Chapter 2 for more information on smart playlists.

Show Song File

If you highlight a song, iTunes will open your computer directory and take you to where the actual song file is stored in your computer memory. Useful if you're trying to locate the actual song file.

Show Current Song

If your iTunes cursor is highlighting a song other than the one playing, selecting this option will highlight the current song playing.

Burn Playlist to Disc

If you have a blank or rewritable CD inside your computer, iTunes will burn your current playlist to the disc. It is the same as the Burn Disc icon in the upper-right corner. See Chapter 2 for more information on burning CDs.

Create an iMix

iTunes lets you post your favorite playlist of songs online through the Apple Music Store. Then your friends and family can create the song list themselves. These are called iMixes.

Update iPod

Apple regularly updates the iPod software with new features and error corrections. This option downloads the latest update to the iPod software for you.

Page Setup

Sets up the parameters for printing your iTunes screen.

Exit

Shut down iTunes.

Edit (PC) or iTunes (Mac)

Here you can cut and paste songs, show duplicates, and set your iTunes preferences. The first set of options is similar to word processing programs such as Microsoft Word.

Undo

Undo the last action.

Cut

Cut the current text.

Copy

Copy the current song or text.

Paste

Place the previously cut or copied text. This also pastes the previously cut or copied song.

Clear

If a song is highlighted, iTunes will remove the song from your library. iTunes will usually ask you if you really want to delete the song before completing the removal.

Select All

Highlight all the songs within the current list.

Select None

Unselect any highlighted items.

Show/Hide Browser

Shows or removes the Browse area above your song list. It's the same as the Browse icon in the upper-right corner. See Chapter 2 to read more about browsing.

Show/Hide Artwork

Shows or removes the album artwork from the lower-left corner of the screen. It does not delete the artwork. See Chapter 2 for more on getting album art.

Show Duplicate Songs

A useful tool, Show Duplicate Songs enables you to see any titles you might have copied twice by mistake. You can then eliminate the duplicates and save space on your computer.

View Options

Here you can select what information you want listed with your music, including year, composer, and times played.

Preferences

This brings up the powerful Preferences menu, from where you can control your iPod options, CD burning techniques, and more. See Chapter 9 for more on preferences.

Controls

From this pull-down menu, you can control functions such as adjust the volume or pause your music. See Chapter 2 for more on playing your music.

Play

Start the current music selection. It is the same as the Play button located in the upper-left corner. See Chapter 2 for more on the Play button.

Next Song

Go to the next music selection. It is the same as the Next button located in the upper-left corner. See Chapter 2 for more on the Next button.

Previous Song

This is a bit of a misnomer. Previous Song "rewinds" the current song selection back to the beginning. Press it twice to go back to the previous music selection. It is the same as the Previous button located in the upper-left corner. See Chapter 2 for more on the Previous button.

Shuffle

Randomizes the play order of your library or current playlist. It is the same as the Shuffle icon, the second icon in the lower-left corner. See Chapter 2 for more on shuffle.

Repeat Off

Don't repeat the library or current playlist when it ends. It is the same as the Repeat icon, the third icon in the lower-left corner. See Chapter 2 for more on repeat.

Repeat All

Start playing the library or current playlist again when you reach the end. It is the same as the Repeat icon, the third icon in the lower-left corner. See Chapter 2 for more on repeat.

Repeat One

Repeat the current song until you say otherwise. It is the same as the Repeat icon, the third icon in the lower-left corner. Click it once to Repeat All, twice for Repeat One (a single song), and three times to return to Repeat Off. See Chapter 2 for more on repeat.

Volume Up

Increase the volume. It is the same as the volume bar located in the upper-left corner. See Chapter 2 for more on volume.

Volume Down

Decrease the volume. It is the same as the volume bar located in the upper-left corner. See Chapter 2 for more on volume.

Mute

Mute the music. You will still hear the usual sounds from your computer.

Eject Disc

Eject the current CD or DVD from your computer. It is the same as the Eject Disc icon in the lower-right corner. See Chapter 2 for more on ejecting discs.

Visualizer

The equivalent of a screen saver, the iTunes Visualizer creates a colorful light show on your monitor. The lights pulsate to the music. Press the Esc key to end the show.

Turn Visualizer On

Starts the show.

Small

Makes the show appear in a small box in the middle of your screen. It is surrounded by a wide black border.

Medium

Makes the show appear in a medium box in the middle of your screen. It is surrounded by a medium black border.

Large

Makes the show appear in a large box in the middle of your screen. It is surrounded by a small black border. Because of the large size, this Visualizer mode may run slow on your computer.

Full Screen

Makes the show appear across the whole screen. Because of the large size, this Visualizer mode may run slow on your computer.

Advanced

Here you'll find a higher level of iTunes control, including radio programming, music authorizations, and conversion.

Switch to Mini Player

Turns your iTunes display into a mini-player consisting of play controls and song information.

Open Stream

Here you can type in a particular live radio show you want to listen to. You only need this if Apple doesn't offer the radio show—otherwise it's easier to click on the Podcasts icon and search for the show. See Chapter 2 for more on radio broadcasts.

Subscribe to Podcast

Here you can type in a particular podcast show you want to subscribe to. You only need this if Apple doesn't offer the show—otherwise it's easier to click on the Podcasts icon and search for the show. See Chapter 10 for more on podcasting.

Convert

Change a song into a different music format, such as MP3, AAC, or WAV. See Chapter 9 on importing to learn more about the iTunes-compatible song formats.

Consolidate Library

If your music is spread across different areas of your computer, use this option to have iTunes put your collection all in one particular file area.

Get CD Track Names

Have iTunes find song data on a commercial CD you've burned on your computer. You need to have an Internet connection for this to work. Read Chapter 2 to learn more about burning.

Submit CD Track Names

Some commercial CDs are too obscure for iTunes to have the song information available. However, you might know the song title, composer, and such. This option enables you to type in the song information and give it to iTunes so that other Apple users can benefit from your knowledge.

Join CD Tracks

Removes the play gaps that usually occur between CD tracks. Highlight the two songs and select this option.

Deauthorize Computer

Disable your computer from purchasing audio-books or music from the Apple Music Store.

Check for Purchased Music

Makes sure that all the music you have purchased has been downloaded onto your iTunes.

Convert ID3 Tags

Music information comes out wrong, particularly if it was imported to your computer by a program other than iTunes. This information is stored in something called an ID3 tag. Highlight the song, select this option, and choose Reverse Unicode. The problem will probably be fixed.

Help

Apple has provided extensive help documents for iTunes. Some require an Internet connection.

iTunes and Music Store Help

Here you can search a help database about iTunes and the Apple Music Store. Type in a particular topic, such as "burning CDs," and it will give you all related tips and tricks. You can also print the information.

iTunes and Music Store Service and Support

This takes you to the Apple help website. Requires an Internet connection.

iPod Help

Here you can search a help database about your iPod. Type in a particular topic, such as "transfer-ring music," and it will give you all related tips and tricks. You can also print the information.

Keyboard Shortcuts

A list of all the keyboard shortcuts you can use instead of pulling down menus or pressing icons.

iTunes Hot Tips

An Apple website with pointers on how to make the best of your iTunes setup. You need Internet access to view.

Shop for iTunes Products

This option takes you to the iPod accessories web-site, where you can purchase the latest iPod prod-ucts. You need Internet access to view. See Chapter 8 to learn more about iPod accessories.

Provide iTunes Feedback

Here you can communicate with Apple. Let them know of a CD that you think should be available through the Apple Music Store, about an error in the music listing, and other kinds of feedback. Apple does not reply in most cases, but the company says that all feedback is noted. You need Internet access to talk with Apple.

Check for iTunes Updates

Touch base with Apple to check for recent iTunes software updates. Apple usually sends you a notice when a new iTunes update is available, but this option is convenient if you happen to miss the message. Internet access is required.

Run CD Diagnostics

iTunes checks the integrity of the current CD or DVD you have in your computer. It gives a short report after a brief spin of the CD drive.

About iTunes

Copyright information.

Index

F

G

H

I-J-K

L–M

N–O

W-X-Y-Z